Life Of Sister St. Rita Of Cascia Of The Order Of St. Augustine

Sister Saint Rita of Cascia

Life of

Sister St. Rita of Cascia

of the

Order of St. Augustine. Advocate of the Impossible.
Model of maidens, wives, mothers, widows and nuns.

Translated by the
Rev. Dan J. Murphy, O. S. A.
From the Spanish of
Rev. Joseph Sicardo, O. S. A.

CHICAGO
D. B. Hansen & Sons
PUBLISHERS

Cum Permissu Superiorum

N. J. MURPHY, O. S. A.,
Provincial

NIHIL OBSTAT
J. F. GREEN, O. S. A.,
Censor Libr.

IMPRIMATUR
GEORGE W. MUNDELEIN, D. D.,
Archbishop, Chicago.

To the
Very Rev. J. F. Green, O. S. A.,
whose pious and untiring zeal has done so much to spread devotion to St. Rita, O.S.A., of Cascia, this volume is affectionately dedicated
By the Translator.

In compliance with the decree of Urban VIII., we hereby assert that we do not intend to attach to the circumstances narrated in this Life any significance other than that belonging to historical facts.

Dan J. Murphy, O. S. A.

CONTENTS

Contents (*Continued*)

PREFACE

The "Lives of the Saints" are only a part, but a precious part of the Library of triumphant Christianity. The catalogue of the "Lives of the Saints" is a long and holy one, so holy, indeed, that it is called a litany, and is used as one of the public prayers of the Catholic Church. On the shelves of this library are found books whose pages relate not only the lives of Jesus Christ, the King of Saints, and of Mary, the Mother of Jesus, the Queen of Saints, but also the story of those pious and holy men and women whose lives were a signal proof that "God is wonderful in His saints." The Church is a faithful custodian of the "Lives of the Saints," of those books which contain the wonderful and glorious deeds of her children who have lived and died in the odor of sanctity. And she looks on every "Life of a Saint" as a guide book pointing out the way to heaven to all Christians who are only travelers on the way to their true home. After the Catechism there is no book more precious to the eyes of Mother Church than a "Life of a Saint." Every age of the Church has had its illustrious saint or saints, and the study of the life of any saint will reveal the providence of God in the government of the world, and especially the divine economy with regard to the children of His Church. Not only are the saints, while living on earth, the glory and ornaments of their birth-lands, but after death their real characters become better known, and Mother Church bestows upon them the highest honors within her power, and, at her command, an entire world gives them their due worship and veneration. It is the dearest wish of Mother Church that her children should frequently read the lives of the saints; by so doing they gradually become acquainted with a select society to which, in a great measure, they will be forced to raise the standard of their daily lives. Our Holy Father St. Augustine is a striking example of what the reading of the lives of the saints may do. A friend of his, Alipius by name, gave him the life of St. Anthony the Abbot. Augustine read it, and was so extremely affected by what he read, that it was one main cause of his conversion. Looking down the long calendar of saints, glancing carefully over the Church's long honor-list of men and women, whose names were talismanic in their days, we find no name crowned with a greater halo of glory and veneration, than that of Sister St. Rita, the humble Augustinian nun of Cascia, now worshiped and venerated under the singular title of the *Saint of the Impossible.* It is more than 450 years since St. Rita departed this life to be united forever to her Lord and spouse Jesus Christ, and yet her name is still held in benediction, not only among the faithful of Italy, her native country, but also among the faithful of the rest of Europe, who vie with the people of South and North America, in honoring and venerating our illustrious Saint. Among the many magnificent "Lives of St. Rita" written by the Italian and Spanish Augustinians, we prefer that written by our brother Religious, Father Joseph Sicardo. As his book has had a large propaganda in Spain, the Philippine Islands and in Spanish America, we have hopes that the same book, garbed in an English dress, will help to keep alive that fire of devotion which now burns in the hearts of so many clients of Sister St. Rita in North America. That our translation of Father Sicardo's "Life of St. Rita" may have the result of further increasing not only the veneration, but also the number of the clients of our Sister St. Rita is our only wish and ambition.

DAN J. MURPHY, O. S. A.

St. Rita's Monastery
Chicago, Ill.
Feast of St. Agatha, 1916.

CHAPTER I.

Umbria, Cascia and Its Greatness.

IF YOU TAKE a glance at the map of Italy, you will observe that the province of Umbria is set, like a gem, in the centre of the Italian peninsula, which has the appearance of an elongated boot dipping down to the Mediterranean Sea.

The capital of Umbria is Perugia, a remarkably beautiful city, situated on a hill on the right of the Tiber. Among its many stately and majestic edifices, Perugia possesses a magnificent cathedral, built in the 14th century, that contains paintings by Barroccio, Manni, and Signorelli. Attached to the cathedral is a valuable library, rich in works and manuscripts, among which is a codex of the Gospel of St. Luke, of the 6th century.

The inhabitants of Umbria are descendants of a long line of ancient and honorable ancestors. They are a God-fearing and God-loving people, and their proudest boast is that they have preserved the faith "once given to the saints."

Travelers and pilgrims, who have visited the province of Umbria, are most emphatic and enthusiastic in praise of this picturesque wonder-land, whose matchless blue skies and delightful climate, its rugged hills and smiling valleys, its fertile soil and its abundance of luscious fruits, are sufficient proofs that bountiful nature has bestowed, with lavish hands, its choicest gifts on this garden spot of the Italian peninsula, whose native charms are the pride and boast of an admiring world. Truly may it be said of Umbria: "Beauty's home is surely there."

If we pass from the order of nature to the order of grace, Umbria becomes a shrine, so to speak, or in other words, a holy land, because it is the birthland of many illustrious saints, whose names are the ornaments of Italy and the glory and honor of the Catholic Church.

What land, under heaven's dome, can lay claim to a galaxy of saints like St. Benedict, St. Francis and St. Clare, both of Assisi? Time has not decreased the holy fame of these saints, on the contrary, time has augmented the glory and veneration of Saints Benedict, Francis and Clare. Their shrines are visited yearly by numerous travelers and pilgrims who are led, not by curiosity, but by an ardent faith, to go and visit the shrines of those holy persons, who, while on earth, were faithful servants of God.

However, the religious glory and fame of Umbria do not rest alone on the trinity of Saints mentioned above. This blessed province is the happy mother of, at least, a dozen saints. The Order of St. Augustine numbers in its long calendar of saints, eight, who claim Umbria as their birthplace, among whom must be specially mentioned: Sister St. Clare of Montefalco and Sister St. Rita of Cascia, called by Leo XIII, of happy memory, *"La perla preziosa de la Umbria"*—*"Umbria's precious pearl."*

About seventy-five miles from Rome, in the southeastern part of Umbria, situated amid hills bordering the Apennines, is the ancient city of Cascia. Cascia was, at one time, the capital of a free and independent republic which consisted of four flourishing cities. Its inhabitants were a brave and sturdy people, and when, in the year 1300, their rights and liberties were threatened by King Robert of Naples, the Cascians, who had tasted the sweets of freedom too long to tamely surrender their liberty, resisted with valor and bravery the King's army. Success crowned their vigorous resistance and the intrepid Cascians won a glorious and decisive victory over their powerful enemies.

There are extant pieces of money, coined when Cascia was at the zenith of its power. On these coins is stamped the escutcheon of Cascia, represented by a young and beautiful maiden, seated on a throne resting on two dragons' heads. The maiden holds a lily in her right hand, and in her left hand a serpent. These same heraldic arms may yet be seen emblazoned on one of the ancient gates which guarded the principal entrance to the once famous city.

In the course of time, evil days fell upon the once happy and prosperous republic. Wars, and especially civil wars, brought disaster and dissension, and where hitherto had reigned peace and prosperity, there began a reign of gloom and despondency. Finding themselves reduced to such an unhappy and miserable condition, and fearful that they would fall under that most terrible of God's judgments—extermination, the inhabitants of Cascia, and their equally unhappy neighbors, placed themselves under the powerful protection of the Blessed Mother of God and became voluntary subjects of the Papal States.

The Cascia of to-day is, so to speak, but a shadow of what it was when "ancient and famous." At present it is but a small town. The number of its inhabitants does not exceed six hundred. Yet small as Cascia is, as regards the number of its people, it has within its walls many monuments, which are living witnesses of the ardent and lively faith of its pious population.

In Cascia there is a beautiful parish-church, dedicated to the Blessed Virgin Mary, and several houses of religious communities. The Augustinian Order has three communities in that little Italian town; one of friars and two of nuns. The friars' monastery, a fine building, is dedicated to our holy founder, St. Augustine. One of the nuns' convents, dedicated formerly to St. Mary Magdalen, is now called St. Rita's convent. The other religious house is dedicated to the glorious Virgin St. Lucy, who suffered martyrdom during the fierce persecution of the cruel and impious Dioclesian.

But though the religious fame and glory of Cascia might safely rest on St. Rita, whose name is a household word in Cascia, still, the archives of that blessed town are the proud possessors of records which mention the names of many holy men, the sanctity of whose lives perfumed, as it were, the moral atmosphere of Cascia. The following are the names of a few of those saintly servants of God, of whom Cascia is the proud mother:

Blessed Giovanni of Castro Clavano.
Blessed Ugolino, O. S. A.
Blessed Simon, O. S. A.
Venerable Andrea of Muciafore, O. S. A.

However, among the many cedars of this Augustinian Lebanon, our Sister St. Rita towers above all others, and the story of her marvellous life, and the many wonderful miracles, wrought through her intercession after death, will convince the reader that God is indeed wonderful in His saints, and that St. Rita, the Augustinian nun of Cascia, is truly, as a venerating world calls her, the *Saint of the Impossible.*

CHAPTER II.

The Birthplace and Parents of St. Rita

ROCCA PORRENA is the name of a small village, or rather hamlet, about three miles from Cascia. It is situated near a small river, in a small valley, at the foot of a high cliff, which, separated from the adjoining mountains, has the appearance of a perfectly formed pine-cone. There is a tradition, that at the time of our Lord's death on the hill of Calvary, an earthquake split the rocks of the mountains in the neighborhood of Cascia, and that this particular cliff remained completely detached from the mountains. On account of its rocky site, Porrena is called Rocca Porrena.

In this small village there lived, about the year 1309, a pious couple who, having plighted their troth at the foot of God's holy altar, consecrated every day of their wedded life to the service of God, and to the practice of those virtues which are most pleasing to God. The names of that worthy couple were Antonio Mancini and Amata Ferri. Antonio was a native of Rocca Porrena; Amata was born at Fogliano, a pretty hamlet, a short distance from Cascia.

Though possessing little of the world's riches, Antonio Mancini earned more than enough, as a tiller of the soil, to enable himself and his good wife to live comfortably. Content with their humble lot, the happy couple felt no poverty, nor did they desire riches, and they gladly distributed to the poor and needy all they did not need for their own support and maintenance. Naturally, such generosity, on the part of Antonio and Amata endeared them to the poor, the lips of many blessed them, and God, who rewards those who help His needy poor, showered His choicest spiritual blessings upon them.

Not only were Antonio and his pious wife generous to the poor and needy, but they were, in very fact, Apostles placed by God in Rocca Porrena, and like Apostles they endeavored to teach their neighbors by word and example, that the only way to save their souls, that the only way to heaven, was by fearing and loving God, as well as by avoiding and shunning sin and vice. The examples of the holy lives of Antonio and Amata, the peace and happiness that reigned in their humble home and the gladness and joy that were ever pictured on their countenances won many, first, to admire and respect them, and then to imitate their holy manner of living. Truly may we say, that the little vine-clad cottage of Rocca Porrena, the humble home of Antonio Mancini and Amata Ferri, must have been a holy and a heavenly home, and were the world blest with more such homes, the world would also be blest with more than one St. Rita.

The true story of the apostolic work of the parents of St. Rita is known to God alone. Nevertheless, one of its chapters has been handed down to us by zealous and trustworthy chroniclers of the Order of St. Augustine. These chroniclers relate, that the home of St. Rita's parents was truly a house of prayer, a sanctuary of holiness, and that their lives were in perfect conformity to the commandments of God and the Church.

They meditated morning and night on the Passion of Jesus Christ, and both had a heartfelt devotion to the ever-blessed Virgin Mary, the Immaculate Mother of God. Antonio and Amata were known, for miles around Rocca Porrena, for their kindness and cheerfulness. Everywhere they went, they cast the radiance of their benevolence, and soothed many an aching heart. In matters of confidence they vied even with the parish-priest. Through their gentle influence family dissensions were healed, and through their prudent advice many indifferent souls were led back to the friendship of God.

Filled with the spirit and grace of God, there was born in the hearts of Antonio Mancini and Amata Ferri the Apostolic zeal of saving souls. They hated and detested sin, but loved the sinner. Hence whenever occasion required it, they discovered a way to approach those who were guilty of grievous sins, without embarrassing or offending them. They reproved them with kindness and continued their gentle reproof, until even the most hardened sinners were moved and learned to hate and be sorry for their sins and hastened to be reconciled with God in the Tribunal of Penance.

Many times when the parents of St. Rita happened to be in the company of some of their neighbors, who, not satisfied with their lot in life, would begin to murmur against the Providence of God, the pious couple would adroitly change the topic of conversation, and speak so feelingly of the Passion of Jesus Christ that their listeners would actually forget their trials and afflictions, and feel ashamed that they had not been willing to suffer a little for Him, who suffered so much for them. Again, when malice, aided by calumny, had kindled the fires of discord, and was fanning the flames of revenge in the hearts of individuals and families, it was then that Antonio Mancini and Amata Ferri employed a holy diplomacy that must have been inspired by heaven. They silenced the voice of calumny, disarmed the desire of revenge, restored harmony among enemies, and even transformed enemies into ardent friends. Such apostolic zeal, such gentleness in reproving sinners, such holy tact in banishing enmity and in settling quarrels and disputes, won for the parents of St. Rita the title: *Peace-makers of Jesus Christ.*

In Rocca Porrena there existed the custom of appointing every year, a man and woman, whose office or function was to settle the disputes and contentions that happened to arise among the inhabitants. This appointment was made on the first Sunday of Lent in the parish-church, and by the parish-priest, who was always very careful to make a prudent appointment. On account of their spotless reputation and well-deserved popularity, it was very natural that Antonio Mancini and his wife Amata were repeatedly appointed the *Peace-makers* of Rocca Porrena; and biographers tell us that their judgments were always accepted as if they were the judgments of God.

Living in the midst of a holy peace and happiness, the fruits of a truly Christian life, there was one joy lacking to the home of Antonio and his spouse. God had sent no child to bless their marriage, and though they had prayed often and fervently for this great blessing, God seemed to be deaf to their prayers. Disappointed, as they naturally were, because their prayers were not answered, they still kept on praying; and even when they had become advanced in years, they redoubled their prayers, so great were their hope and confidence in God. God rewarded their hope and confidence and bestowed on Amata Mancini the same favor He had bestowed on Anna, the mother of Samuel, and on Elizabeth, the mother of St. John the Baptist.

One night, while Amata was praying in her humble home, an angel appeared to her, in a vision, and told her that it was the will of God that there would be born of her a daughter who would be, from her very birth, marked with the seal of sanctity, gifted with every virtue, and that she was to be a helper of the helpless, an advocate of the afflicted, and a guiding star in the firmament of the Church. Amata was consoled and made happy by the words of the angel, and when she told the glad news to her husband Antonio, both joined in a heart-felt prayer of thanksgiving to God, who was pleased to bless their old age with such a signal favor.

CHAPTER III.

St. Rita's Birth

FILLED with unspeakable joy and gladness, that God had deigned to look upon her with mercy, from the evening the angel made known to Amata Mancini that she had found grace with God, and was to become a mother both she and her husband Antonio spent their days, and the greater part of their nights, in close communication with God, awaiting the happy event. At length the time came, when the little hamlet of Rocca Porrena, the least, indeed, of all the hamlets of Umbria, was to become famous as the birthplace of a child, who, in after years, was to be known and venerated as a great saint and servant of God. The biographers of St. Rita give the day, date and year of her birth, as Saturday, May 22nd, in the year of our Lord 1381, during the pontificate of Pope Urban VI.

Words cannot describe the indescribable joy of Antonio and Amata, as, with loving eyes, they gazed on their little daughter whom they considered a precious gift of God, the fruit of their desires, and the reward of their long years of hope and confidence in God. The unexpected news, that Amata Mancini had become a mother in her old age, was the cause of much surprise, talk, and gossip among the inhabitants of Rocca Porrena. All considered the event as truly miraculous.

Every man, woman, and grown-up child of the little hamlet went to offer congratulations to the happy and overjoyed parents, and all, who gazed on the smiling face of the new-born babe, were charmed by the radiance of the little one's wonderful beauty.

A few days after the happy delivery of Amata, she desired that her little daughter be baptized, and both parents began to consider what name to give her. While pondering over the choice of a name, God made known to the pious parents that it was His wish, that their babe should be named Rita. Accordingly on the fourth day after her birth, the child of Antonio Mancini and Amata Ferri was baptized in St. Mary's, the parish-church of Cascia, there being, at that time, no baptismal font in the church at Rocca Porrena. As was commanded by God, the little babe was baptized Rita, a name till then unknown to the world, but since that time the sweet name of Rita has been given to many Catholic babes, when they are made children of God, and heirs of the kingdom of heaven, by the regenerating waters of the Sacrament of Baptism.

Some authors, who have written the life of our saint, claim that she received, at her baptism, the name of Margarita, and that Rita is a contraction of Margarita. But though we know that the practice of contracting or syncopating names, and especially the names of women, is very common in Italy, we follow the opinion of the learned Augustinian writer, Didacus, who tells us that the child of Antonio Mancini and Amata Ferri was baptized Rita. And furthermore, we read in the Decree of the Canonization of our Saint, that it was announced to Amata, in a vision, that she should call her child Rita.

Shortly after Rita had been regenerated by the saving waters of Baptism, God attested, by a singular prodigy, that her name was not of human invention, but rather of heavenly origin. The day after her Baptism, the fifth after her birth, a swarm of bees, white as the driven snow, was noticed hovering and buzzing around the sweet angelic face of the little Rita, as she lay quietly sleeping in her cradle. The bees alighted on her lips and were seen to enter and issue forth from her partially opened mouth, without harming her, or causing her to awaken from her slumber. All who were witnesses of this singular prodigy recognized that it implied a mystery, though they could not understand or fathom its meaning. In after years, Rita herself made known the meaning of the mystery, by the singular sweetness and simplicity of her manner, and by the eminent sactity of her marvellous life, of which the swarm of white bees that buzzed around the cradle of her infancy was a happy presage. The bees were also a mysterious presage of Rita's future Beatification that was to take place when the bees of Urban VIII reigned in the Church.

Concerning these mysterious bees we must observe. The prodigy, after four centuries, still exists in the small swarm of bees that now dwell in a small fissure in the convent wall, midway between the cell St. Rita occupied and the place of her sepulchre. Their color is not white, as some authors have said, confounding these bees with those that appeared at her cradle. Their color is that of the common bee, except the back, which is a dark red, and they have no sting. They live retired the greater part of the year, but they leave their tiny abode during the last few days of Holy Week and return for the feast of St. Rita. On one occasion, one of these bees was sent to Urban VIII enclosed in a glass vase. It remained, however, but one day in the Pope's palace, and returned, at once, to its companions in Cascia. We will close this chapter by saying: Catholic mothers have rocked the cradles of many remarkable babes, but none more remarkable than that of our little sister—Rita of Rocca Porrena.

CHAPTER IV.

THE EARLY YEARS OF ST. RITA.

INNOCENCE and purity are sister virtues, or at least they are inseparable companions. Where innocence is, there also is purity. In fact, innocence and purity are so intimately associated that they appear to be one and the same virtue. Though natural to infancy, the exercise of these two virtues is the effect of divine grace.

Guided by the wisdom from above, Antonio Mancini and Amata Ferri, the pious parents of St. Rita, watched, with loving and jealous care, over every day of her infancy, for they regarded their little babe as a gift from heaven, the fruit of a special grace, and the child of God rather than of man. Hence we may safely say, without any fear of exaggeration, that little Rita Mancini began to be a saint and to live a supernatural life, from the very moment of her Baptism, when her soul was made beautiful by divine grace. And that the virtues of innocence and purity were deeply rooted in her pure soul, for scarcely had she come to use of reason, than she became the possessor of an innocence and a purity which were really marvellous in one of so tender an age. These two virtues were mirrored on her angelic face. Her every word exhaled an odor of sweetness, and possessed a mysterious power which inclined the soul to God; while her every act bespoke the guidance of a power far above the human. Little Rita was indeed, so to speak, a precious plant, planted, as it were, by the hands of God in His vineyard, and with loving care did God cause the dews of heavenly grace to fall gently on that tender plant, which was to become in later years, and we may say for all years, a towering cedar of His glory and omnipotence. Clothed, therefore, as our little sister was, with the double cloak of innocence and purity, her guardian angel, who was ever by her side, took her by the hand and led his little companion along the most prudent paths, nor did God permit her to perform any act, or entertain any thought, but those compatible with His holy will and service.

It is not, therefore, a matter of surprise, that the little servant of God differed from other children in her early years, for at the age when most children are accustomed to enjoy and amuse themselves, with dolls and other playthings, little Rita Mancini found no pleasure in child-games or child-toys. You must not think, however, that little Rita did not associate with children of her own age; on the contrary, she had scores of little friends among the children of Rocca Porrena, and though she did not, as a rule, engage in their games, nevertheless, she took pleasure in seeing her little friends enjoy themselves. Even when she grew larger, instead of desiring to be present at picnics or parties where little girls experience great joy in being admired and petted by relatives and friends, the little Rita preferred solitude to these mirthful gatherings, and many a time when her loving mother wished to dress her, according to the fashion of the day, she would hie to a remote corner of the house, to pray and contemplate the divine mysteries, particularly the Passion of Jesus Christ, a devotion she had inherited from her pious parents.

We must not judge from little Rita's dislike to be clad in pretty frocks and dresses, that she was at times wilful and disobedient; on the contrary, she was a most obedient child, she loved dearly her aged parents, and many and many a time did she kneel at her mother's knees, listening to her holy counsels, after the manner of the little immaculate Mary of Nazareth at the knees of her mother St. Anne. Hence what may have seemed disobedience, on the part of little Rita, were in fact mild reproofs, prompted, no doubt, by God, against that vanity which alas, too often is planted by indulgent parents, in the hearts of their young children.

One of little Rita's chief delights was to go to church with her parents, and when she entered the house of God, she sought the most retired place, where she recited with devotion the Angelical Salutation which she knew by heart, and then, as if God had given His little servant a clear understanding of the Incarnation of our Lord, she would close her eyes, and give her whole soul to a deep contemplation of this great mystery. Oftentimes, while assisting at the holy sacrifice of the Mass, her face would change its expression. Sometimes it bore the expression of glad joy, and at other times, her face would indicate that she was experiencing moments of sadness. These alternate expressions of gladness and sadness plainly told how glad she was to be in the house of God kneeling in the presence of Jesus in the Blessed Sacrament, and how sad she became at the very thought that her innocent Jesus was obliged to die an ignominious death on the wood of the Cross. Oh, would that we, who assist so often at the holy Sacrifice of the

Mass, could experience, in our hearts and souls, the same spiritual joy and sadness!

We must also observe that little Rita had a great love and affection for the poor. At table, whenever her mother put on her plate a portion of the family meal, one portion she ate herself, the other portion she preserved to give to some poor child of the neighborhood. This practice was habitual with the little Rita, and it is certain she felt more happiness in giving away a portion of her meals, than in eating what she retained for herself.

The people of Rocca Porrena, when they saw how different Rita Mancini was from the other children of the hamlet, and when they observed that as she grew in years, her life became more holy and sacramental, they respected and revered her, not indeed as a child, but rather as a person grown old in virtue. Especially were the mothers of Rocca Porrena edified by her holy and exemplary child-life, and they were continually telling their little daughters to take Rita Mancini as their model.

The fame of little Rita's holy life was not limited to the narrow zone of Rocca Porrena, it became known and was spoken of in many of the towns and villages of Umbria; but especially did the inhabitants of her humble birthplace rejoice, for they were beginning to see realized what was predicted at her cradle by the swarm of white bees, which, like flakes of snow, entered and issued from her sweet mouth; for the child-life of St. Rita was so celestial, that she appeared to be a little angel living in the world, yet immune from all its imperfection and corruption.

CHAPTER V.

St. Rita Begins to Lead a Life of Retirement, and Desires Ardently to Consecrate Her Virginity to God

GOD is, indeed, wonderful in His saints, and a careful study of the life of St. Rita of Cascia, from her cradle to the grave, will convince anyone of this beautiful and holy truth. Already a model of innocence and purity, and though as yet but a child, it was Rita's ardent desire to live a solitary life in some hidden cave or grotto, where she might pass her days uninterrupted in prayer and contemplation, because she coveted to be alone with God. Filial love, however, and the obedience due her aged parents whom she felt would oppose this, hindered the execution of her holy desire.

Not a little disappointed, but by no means discouraged, she wavered not in her determination to live in retirement, so that she might be as near as possible to God. How to succeed in this determination, and at the same time be submissive to her parents, was for Rita a perplexing problem. Her perplexity, however, was of short duration. God, who must have regarded with rapture the pure and innocent heart of His young servant, inspired her to build a small but pretty oratory in a retired part of her home, where she remained for one whole year, separated from all commerce with the world, unless we except her parents, to whom she spoke only when necessary. During that year of solitude, Rita spent her time meditating on the sorrowful mysteries of the Passion of Jesus Christ. And, as a help to her meditation, she had painted on the walls of her little oratory some scenes of the life of Christ; such as, the crib wherein the infant Jesus was laid after His birth; Mount Calvary, the theatre of His death on the Cross; and the sepulchre wherein His sacred body was placed, after it had been taken down from the Cross. It is also probable that a picture of the Blessed Mother of Jesus ornamented the walls of her oratory. Gazing at those pictures, she experienced no distractions in her prayers or meditations, but true as the steel to the magnet, her heart and soul were so attracted by Jesus Christ, that she desired nothing more than to have and possess the love and grace of her crucified Lord.

At the conclusion of that year, spent, for the most part, in constant prayer and commerce with God and His mother, Rita saw that her parents needed her constant aid and assistance, especially her mother.

Antonio Mancini, once robust and vigorous, had become so feeble that it was with great difficulty he cultivated a small garden, which supplied his frugal table with vegetables; and his faithful wife Amata, whose age had debilitated and sapped her strength, could only perform a small part of the ordinary household duties. Rita, who understood thoroughly the obligations of children towards their parents, judged it to be the will of God that she should give up her retired life, so that it might not be, in any way, a hindrance to her duty towards her aged father and mother. Accordingly, Rita came forth from the retreat where she had spent so many days and nights with God, and became, to the great joy of her parents, the housekeeper, so to speak, of her humble home.

How well Rita performed the duties of housekeeper, we may surmise. And it must have pleased her parents, especially her mother, to see how industrious and painstaking their little daughter was, as, like an angel, in human form, she busied herself while at work. But though Rita was most assiduous about her work, it never seemed to interfere or interrupt her prayer, not withstanding her extreme attention to her exterior employments, she acquired a wonderful facility of joining them with mental prayer, and of keeping herself constantly in the presence of God, who, no doubt, aided His little hand-maid with her work, and guided her little hands to make and keep the humble home of her parents a model of order and neatness. Would that the children of the present day loved and obeyed their parents as did little Rita Mancini! Then would be silenced forever that complaint of so many fathers and mothers: "I have lost control of my children."

Having spent a few years employed in the duties of housekeeper, Rita arrived at that age, when young girls, especially in Italy, are accustomed to choose their future state in life. From the Augustinian breviary we learn that Rita Mancini was twelve years of age when she made her choice. She consulted no one but God, and as it was her one desire to consecrate her virginity to God, so that she might better preserve the candor of her soul, of which the white bees that hovered around her cradle were the heralds, she determined to be a true spouse of Christ, by embracing a religious life, and become a nun. But alas, many years were to pass before Rita's aspirations were fulfilled, for, by the permission of God, it was only after being tried in the crucible of afflictions and contradictions, that she found, at last, that happiness for which her heart yearned from the time she was but a child.

Having resolved to become a spouse of Jesus Christ, and to dedicate herself wholly to His service, Rita's first thought, as became an obedient daughter, was to make known her determination to her parents and obtain their permission. Accordingly, one evening, when her father and mother were talking together, Rita, who had been an attentive listener to their pious and holy conversation, waited until they finished. She then kissed them both reverently, and told them that she had made up her mind to become a nun.

Antonio Mancini and Amata Ferri were overcome with surprise, and their old and wrinkled countenances became clouded with sadness, at what their young daughter had told them. And as she continued, with humility and with an eloquence that was more than human, to plead for their permission, every word that Rita uttered pierced, like sharp arrows, the hearts of her parents and even brought tears to their eyes. And yet, because Rita loved her parents, and would not do anything to cause them the least sorrow or pain, there were included in her holy plea, the words of submission and resignation: "Not my will, dear parents, but thine be done."

The silence that followed Rita's earnest plea for her parents' permission to permit her to embrace the religious state, caused her to divine that her parents had just reasons for not granting her desire. At length when her parents could no longer hide their sorrow, they broke silence, and, betwixt sobs and sighs, spoke feelingly to Rita. They reminded her that they were already advanced in years; that she was their only child, and, after God, their solace, comfort and support; and finally they said, that through her, they hoped to see their family saved from extinction. The tears and pleading of Antonio and Amata were not fruitless. Hitherto Rita had never disobeyed her parents. In fact, it had been her custom to anticipate their wishes. But, on this occasion, no one but God will ever know how much, and what it cost Rita Mancini, when she told her parents that she would obey their will and remain at home to comfort and assist their old age. Nevertheless, though love and obedience prevented Rita from embracing the religious state, she was firmly determined to remain a faithful spouse of her divine bridegroom, Jesus Christ, to whom, in her heart, she had pledged her fidelity.

CHAPTER VI.

St. Rita Sacrifices Her Will on the Altar of Obedience, and Consents to Enter the Marriage State

WE HAVE related in the last chapter, that Rita, yielding to the tears and supplications of her aged parents, promised to remain at home to comfort and assist them. Her promise, however, did not, in any way, weaken her determination to preserve inviolate the flower of her virginity, which she already desired to consecrate to God. But seeing that there was little hope of embracing the religious state, at least, while her parents lived, so inflamed was she with the love of Jesus Christ and the most glorious Virgin Mary, that she resolved never to embrace the married state. Having made this resolution, a double joy and consolation filled the heart of Rita; she could remain faithful to her divine Bridegroom, and, at the same time be a loving and obedient daughter. By reason of this double joy and consolation, a heavenly light illumined continually her countenance, and, as she performed, day in and day out, her domestic duties, she cast a halo of happiness everywhere around her.

But Rita's joy and happiness were of short duration. Her filial love and obedience were to be put to a further test, a test that was to cause in her soul, a real combat between her love of God, and the love of her parents. Antonio Mancini and Amata Ferri, overjoyed that their daughter had given up the idea of entering a convent, now determined that she should enter the marriage state. They had already hinted that this was their wish, when they had persuaded their young daughter, that she was duty-bound not to abandon them. It is certain, however, that in yielding to the entreaties of her parents not to enter a convent, it had never entered into the mind of Rita to have any spouse other than Jesus Christ. We can, therefore, imagine, first, the surprise and then the inexpressible anguish to which Rita became a prey, when her parents told her, they were going to choose a husband for her, as it was their wish that she should marry. Their age added eloquence to their words as they insisted that she should consent to their wishes. They reminded her that she had been given to them in their old age, long after they had almost given up all hope of offspring, and they emphasized, that she, by her marriage, would be the cause, not only of saving their family from extinction, but also of making their declining years happy and comfortable. We would, indeed, be tempted to condemn Antonio Mancini and his wife Amata for arrogating to themselves the right to force the vocation of their daughter, and thus making her the prey of human calculation, did we not believe that God, in His profound and impenetrable wisdom, permitted this, so that His chosen servant Rita, after having been a model for Christian maidens, should also, like Saint Monica, become a model for Christian wives and mothers.

The unexpected announcement of her parents wrung tears from the eyes of Rita, and nearly broke her heart. A sort of paralysis seized her, and for some moments she could not find her voice. When the martyrdom that was taking place in her pure soul had somewhat subsided, Rita recovered the use of her tongue, and firmly but with dove-like simplicity, said: "My parents, I do not wish any spouse but Jesus Christ. Years ago I dedicated my whole body, heart and soul to His love and holy service. Becuase you wished it, I gave my promise not to enter a convent. I feel sure, with the help of God, without embracing the marriage state, that I will be able to console and comfort you, and provide for all your necessities, until God calls you to a better and a happier home."

But Antonio and Amata, who had made up their minds that their daughter should marry, turned deaf ears to the heartfelt words of Rita, and the poor child, judging that further speech would be useless, in her desire to be alone with God, retired from the presence of her parents, and hurried to the solitude and quiet of her beloved oratory. Once within its walls, she fell upon her knees, and raising her eyes, with hope and confidence, to the crucifix, asked her crucified Lord to relieve her of that poignant perplexity which had begun to tear her very heart, from the moment her parents told her that it was their will that she should marry. She also implored the Queen of Angels and Virgins, and asked her to be so kind as to obtain for her from God the lights which were necessary for accomplishing what would prove most acceptable to His divine majesty, and conducive to her soul's salvation, expressing to her merely the ardent desire she felt of embracing on earth an angelic mode of life.

Without any doubt, Rita knew it would be no sin to marry in obedience to the will of her parents, but since she felt that God had called her, even from her early years, to be His spouse, and since she had responded generously to this summons, by desiring to vow to God the jewel of her virginity, Rita now awaited on bended knees the voice and decision of God, which would tell her if she should and could obey the will of her parents without offending the will of her Jesus whom she loved with her whole heart and soul.

It is very certain that the fervent prayers which Rita offered in her little oratory were graciously heard by God, who soothed and consoled her aching and troubled heart. And we may believe that God made known to His servant Rita, that she should conform and submit her will to the will of her parents, and that by so doing, she would obey His holy will, without losing any of the merits already gained by the ardent desire of consecrating her virginity to Him, as the sole Lord and Spouse of her heart and soul.

As soon as Rita had learned that it was the will of God that she should submit to the will of her parents, and that she would please God more by her submission than by following her own will, she resolved, then and there, to obey the voice and will of God, and offer no further opposition to the will and desires of her parents. Accordingly, Rita returned to her parents, and prostrating herself at their feet, humbly asked pardon for the repugnance she had hitherto manifested to their will, and told them she was disposed and willing to embrace whatever state of life they wished her to enter.

CHAPTER VII.

St. Rita's Marriage

ANTONIO MANCINI and Amata Ferri, happy with joy because their daughter had consented to enter the marriage state, began, at once, the search for a suitable husband for Rita. A model of children, because her childhood was most remarkable, she became the model of maidens, when she stepped across the threshold that separates childhood from maidenhood. Beautiful as an angel, modest as innocence and lovable as virtue, Rita Mancini could have had, if she wished, many suitors for her hand. All who saw her could not help being attracted by her physical beauty, and all who knew her were charmed by her native modesty, both in conduct and speech. In a word, Rita Mancini was esteemed and respected by every one with whom she came in contact. We can easily believe, that among the many exemplary and industrious young men of Rocca Porrena there were more than one who would have gladly chosen Rita as wife, but since we know that from her earliest years, her sole desire was to have no other lover but Jesus Christ, we can well understand why she had no desire to keep company with the opposite sex.

But now the time had come when Rita Mancini was to enter a new state in life. She had yielded to the insistence of her aged parents, and had consented to marry whomsoever they would choose for her husband. That Rita's choice would have been a different and a better one than that of her parents, we have no doubt. But Rita had no voice in the matter, for Antonio Mancini and his wife Amata selected for their future son-in-law, a young man whose name was Ferdinando. The early biographers of St. Rita tell us that Ferdinando was the son of well-to-do and influential parents. He was gifted with excellent parts, but proud and haughty, surly in speech, and by no means a religious man.

There is no doubt but that Ferdinando, who was the very opposite in character and disposition to the modest and gentle Rita, felt highly honored, when he learned from her parents that he was the only one, among all the young men of Rocca Porrena, who might pay court to their daughter with the view of leading her to the altar as his bride. Ferdinando proved himself an ardent wooer, and after a short courtship, he and Rita pledged their marriage vows before the altar of God, in the presence of Jesus Christ in the Blessed Sacrament. The marriage of Ferdinando and Rita recalls to our mind the marriage of St. Monica, the mother of the illustrious St. Augustine. She was married under circumstances similar to those of St. Rita, and like St. Rita, has bequeathed to posterity a sacred name and memory, both written with letters of gold in the annals of the Catholic Church.

Ferdinando and Rita spent the days of their honeymoon, as is the custom in Italy, visiting and enjoying themselves among relatives and friends. Outwardly, Rita appeared to be happy. She shook hands with all who approached to offer congratulations, and acknowledged with a sweet smile the many good wishes that were showered upon her. But her heart and soul took no part in the festivities that were going on around her; for do what she would, she could not help shedding tears at the very thought of losing that pearl of earthly happiness, which she had sought to give and consecrate solely to God.

Rita had been married but a very short time, when Ferdinando began to show his true character, and Rita began to experience that her marriage was an apprenticeship to trials and sorrows. Words cannot describe the almost inhuman conduct of Ferdinando with regard to his wife Rita. When he spoke, his words were always harsh and cruel. Like the sea that is agitated by the least motion of the wind, Ferdinando flew into a passion at everything that Rita said, or at everything she did, so that instead of her companion and protector, he was in very fact her relentless persecutor.

Under the weight and strain of such persecution, and we may call it martyrdom, many a young wife would have succumbed under the ordeal, but not so Rita. She suffered the unnatural treatment of her cruel husband with a surprising courage and fortitude, and aided by God, who gave her the grace of suffering, she gave a most signal example of patience and humility.

Armed with these two eminent virtues, Rita set to work to reform and conquer the sullen and perverse disposition of Ferdinando. Well trained, from her early years in the art of housekeeping, she helped her maids perform the household duties, with the utmost care and diligence, and was most untiring in her efforts to make, as only a good wife can, the home of her husband an earthly paradise. In her endeavors to check the wild rage of his anger, she sometimes observed a strict silence, uttering not a single word. At other times she performed with humility whatever he commanded her to do, and very often answered him when forced to do so, with words of holiness and sweetness such as angels use.

But alas, the ugly and morose character of Ferdinando, instead of becoming less rude and sullen, became more and more an instrument of torture to Rita's patience, a patience as praiseworthy and laudable as that of holy Job. For if God permitted that His servant Job should suffer great temporal losses, as well as the calumnies of his best friends, and even of his own wife, so that his patience might be, for all ages, a shining example, we may also say the same as regards the sufferings and patience of St. Rita. When she plighted her troth to Ferdinando she thought he would be both a loving husband and a kind companion. But instead, he proved himself a cruel enemy who continually mortified and tortured her. He dissipated, and squandered much of his money at gaming, and though he gave Rita more than enough money for the household expenses, he was always complaining that she was extravagant. He insulted her time and again with injurious and scurrilous words, and sometimes, perhaps, laid violent hands upon her defenseless body. But Rita suffered all this cruel treatment with heroic patience, because it was the will of God that she should become a mirror of patience, by means of which she was the beloved of God, and loved and revered by men.

In closing this chapter, we may say with truth, that God placed St. Rita in His church and made her both a mirror and a flaming torch, so that married women may see in her and learn from her example, how to suffer with fortitude and patience, the bad conduct and cruel treatment of bad and perverse husbands.

CHAPTER VIII.

St. Rita, by Her Humility and Patience, Converts Her Cruel Husband

THERE is in the character of each of the great saints of the Augustinian Order, a peculiar trait or virtue that attracts, in a special manner, our attention and admiration. In St. Augustine, we find a burning love for penance after his memorable conversion; in St. Monica, we discover a remarkable love of prayer; in St. Thomas of Villanova, we cannot help observing his extreme charity for the poor and needy; in St. Clare of Montefalco, we are moved by her great devotion to the Passion of Jesus Christ; but when we come to speak of St. Rita of Cascia, though she possessed, in an eminent degree, the virtues for which her spiritual brothers and sisters are distinguished, we must say, that it is chiefly on account of her God-like love of humility and patience, that she merits our unstinted respect and veneration. And we shall see in the course of this chapter, that it was by reason of the exercise of these two virtues, that she converted her cruel husband from his wicked ways, and made her home a peaceful sanctuary of holy bliss.

As we related in the last chapter, Ferdinando, the husband of Rita, did all he could, by his wicked and perverse conduct, to make her life miserable and unhappy. But like the valiant woman she was, she rendered him good and not evil. Mindful of the promises she made at the foot of the altar, Rita humbly obeyed her husband with extraordinary punctuality and zeal. Of a most retiring disposition, instead of visiting or gossiping with the women of the neighborhood, she remained at home, never leaving it, except to pay a visit to her aged parents, or to go to Mass or Vespers. But never did she go anywhere, without acquainting her husband, or asking his permission. She paid much attention to the comfort of Ferdinando, and took zealous care that his clothes were always scrupulously neat. The management of her household was wise and prudent, and to teach with example what she advocated with words, she clothed herself with modest raiment, not having the least desire for costly and stylish dresses or any kind of ornaments. For Rita knew well, that all the beauty of the King's daughter is within. She was kind and affable to the domestics of her household, and studied to make them happy and contented with their lot. She saw that they attended their religious duties, taught them good and polite manners, and moulded them into models of obedience, neatness and propriety. So much so indeed, that her neighbors were accustomed to tell their domestics that they should take pattern from those of Rita. And it was a common saying in Rocca Porrena, that as Rita Mancini had been a model of a perfect maiden, she was indeed a model of a perfect wife.

What a pity, we are inclined to say, that Rita, who carried sunshine and holiness as an atmosphere, had to undergo so many trials and sufferings. And yet, in spite of those trials and sufferings, she, so to speak, by making use of the trowel of humility and the mortar of patience, laid the corner-stone and builded the foundation, on which was erected that splendid edifice of domestic peace that won the admiration and encomiums of her neighbors.

We know that from the very beginning of her married life, her husband Ferdinando was an obstacle to that peace. But Rita met his opposition with the arms of humility and patience which experience had taught her to handle with skill and precision. Whenever her husband became angry, she studied to sweeten his temper; sometimes by silence, and indeed her silence was a wordless prayer that ascended to heaven; and at other times she waited until his fit of anger was over, and then she would try with sweet and holy words, to reason with him, and make him understand, how great was his offense against God, and how little he thought of his intelligence, to allow himself to become the prey and the slave of anger and passion.

This manner of acting, on the part of Rita, had a great and beneficial effect on her husband, and many a time after she had mildly upbraided him, for yielding to anger and using injurious words, he would become somewhat embarrassed and actually ashamed of himself, and would rush from the house and not return until he became fully calm and recollected.

As time went by, Rita observed with joy that Ferdinando was beginning to be less choleric and less cruel in his manner of speaking and acting towards her. Her humility and patience, supplemented by prayers and tears softened his fierce and almost ungovernable temper, and God opened his eyes and made him see and understand, what a cruel husband he had been to persecute and torment a wife, who bore and tolerated his angry and injurious words, with the meekness of a dove, who served him with humility; who respected him when he himself had lost all respect; and who obeyed him, when obedience cost her much suffering and many humiliations.

Ferdinando became at length a changed man. He saw, as in a vision, what manner of man he had been, and was truly pentitent. He confessed with a sorrowful heart, that blinded by passion, he had been an ungrateful and cruel husband. He frequently returned thanks to God, for having given him as a wife, so good and exemplary a woman as Rita, who by her humility and patience, had led him from the paths of wickedness and disorder onto the paths of virtue and peace, thereby making him faithful to all the duties of a good husband and a devout Christian.

Peace and harmony being established between Ferdinando and Rita, their household became a garden of paradise. Words of prayer and kindness were constantly on the lips of Ferdinando, instead of angry, threatening and abusive utterances. At home, he was kindness itself, and showered every kind of loving attention on Rita; and abroad, he could not find words enough to praise her virtues and worth. On her part Rita was extremely happy, and was untiring in her thanksgiving to God, for having aided in converting her husband from being a raging lion into a faithful and loving husband and as docile as a lamb. No wonder an admiring world places St. Rita of Cascia side by side with St. Monica, as the model of Christian wives.

CHAPTER IX.

God Blesses the Marriage of St. Rita With Two Beautiful Children

SCARCELY had Rita begun to enjoy the fruits of Ferdinando's conversion, than a new sorrow came upon her. Her aged father and mother died and passed to their reward in heaven. Rita felt and mourned their death, not only because she loved them with the deepest affection, but also because she considered them her instructors who gave her the first lessons in piety, and taught her to walk in the way of Christian perfection. But this sorrow was soon lessened, for God, in His mercy and goodness, sent her a great blessing that filled her heart and soul with gladness and joy.

During the several unhappy years that followed the marriage of Ferdinando and Rita Mancini, years signalized by the unchristian life and cruel conduct of Ferdinando, and the prayers, tears and trials of Rita, God had not deigned to bless their union with offspring. This great blessing, however, was not to be denied to Rita, it was only delayed. God, it would seem, was waiting until she converted her husband from his evil ways, and made him worthy to receive from His hands, that gift which, to a married couple, is the most precious and the most welcome of all gifts—a little child.

That Rita, in her hours of sadness and affliction, mourned the absence of a little one to fondle and caress; of a tiny baby-mouth to kiss; of a little crib over which she could softly sing a lullaby, we are inclined to believe. But this absence never caused Rita to murmur against the will of God; on the contrary, it often prompted her to say: *Sia fatta la volunta di Dio. May the will of God be done.* This short prayer of holy resignation was heard in heaven, and after Rita had established peace in her home by winning Ferdinando to a sense of his Christian duties, God sent her two beautiful children to be, as it were, pledges that guaranteed the peace and happiness and love of both her husband and herself.

The birth of their first child, who received, at the baptismal font, the name of Giovanni, naturally filled the hearts of Ferdinando and Rita with joy and gladness, and many and fervent were the thanksgiving prayers that both recited by the cradle-side of their little son, whom God had sent to bless their home. Especially was Ferdinando happy, for he saw in his little son Giovanni the promise of the preservation of his family and name. A name that was an honorable one, though he himself had besmirched it, time and again, before he had come under the benign influence of his saintly and holy wife.

As regards Rita, there was no happier mother in Rocca Porenna, and we may say in all Italy. Her heart now bestowed its love and affection impartially on her little son and his father. And, no doubt, she would have wished for no more happiness in this world, were there not always before her mind the vision of a convent with its little cell, wherein she was to find a still greater happiness, after she had fulfilled, according to the will of God, the honorable and sacred duties of wife and mother.

With joy and happiness perfuming, so to speak, the atmosphere of her home, and the white dove of peace hovering around the hearth of Rita, we can easily fancy what a pretty picture of domestic bliss Ferdinando and Rita made, as they sat by the cradle of their little son vying in love and affection for their *Angioletto,* a term of endearment they were wont to call their little Giovanni. When the little Giovanni was but a few days more than a month, his parents carried him to the church, where they offered him to God, and asked God to aid them to bring him up according to His holy will.

But in the designs of God's providence, a new happiness awaited the already happy Ferdinando and Rita, and, in God's own time, their happiness was duplicated. Rita gave birth to a second child, who was baptized Paulo. Like his little brother Giovanni, Paulo was offered to God, and now Ferdinando and Rita had four little feet to guide on the path to heaven instead of two. The education of Giovanni and Paulo began in the lap of their mother, and, between kisses and caresses, the first word she taught them to pronounce was that sweetest of all sweet names—*the Holy Name of Jesus.* As Giovanni and Paulo advanced in years, Rita taught them to pray, and used every method to prevent the first sallies of dangerous passions, and impressed upon their young minds, the priceless value of humility and patience, those beautiful virtues, of which Rita herself was a most striking example.

What a beautiful school did not Rita establish, and what an excellent course of studies did she not plan for the education of her two sons! Without neglecting to instruct them in profane knowledge, she paid particular attention to educate them in the science of salvation. Ferdinando aided also in the education of his sons by setting them good examples, for he had also been taught by Rita, that good example is like an inheritance given by a parent to a son, an almost infallible means of conveying the virtues of one to the other.

As a result of Rita's teaching, she, who began to be a saint from the very moment of her Baptism, made saints of her children. She and her husband had the happiness to see Giovanni and Paulo grow up to be young boys, truthful, obedient and respectful, indifferent to the things of the world, with the greatest ardor for virtue, the greatest love for God, fear of his judgments and dread of sin. What a happy and holy world it would be, if there were more mothers like St. Rita of Cascia.

CHAPTER X.

The Virtues That St. Rita Practiced During Her Married Life

ST. RITA demonstrated clearly, during the whole course of her married life, that the practice of virtue is not incompatible with the holy state of matrimony. St. Rita did more. She practiced, to a high degree, those virtues that shine most resplendent in the higher state of life, and what is most surprising, she practiced them without experiencing the least obstacle in doing so. The secret of St. Rita's facility in the practice of virtue was, she kept herself at all times and in all places in the grace and presence of God. She was all for God, and everything she said or did was for the honor and glory of God. Hence the more urgent were the obligations of her state of life, the more she felt herself disposed to the practice of virtue; for she judged that she would not be sufficiently grateful for all the graces and favors He had bestowed upon her, if, besides practicing the virtues peculiar to the marriage state, she did not practice those which belonged to the higher state.

St. Rita was indeed well prepared to practice any and every virtue, for the lamp of her soul was filled with the oil of good works, after the manner of the lamps of the prudent virgins made mention of in the

Gospel, and she was in no way inferior to them. The miraculous incorruptibility of her body and the sweet odor which it exhales even to this day, plainly tell us, that St. Rita did not lose any of the reward that God gives to virgins, though she, by virtue of obedience to the wishes of her parents and guided by the will of God, did embrace the married state.

In this chapter we will only speak of a few of the virtues which St. Rita practiced during her married life. To say even a few words of the many virtues she possessed would require a volume by itself. For her soul was endowed with as many virtues, and clothed and decked with as many ornaments of grace, as that woman of strength and beauty, whose picture has been painted by the Holy Ghost, and of which picture St. Rita is a faithful copy.

Our saint was, as it were, a fragrant rose, who preserved, amidst the thorns of penance, her conjugal chastity. Although she never committed a grievous fault, she punished her innocent body with the discipline, and kept it under the complete control of the spirit, by continual fastings. Not content with observing the fast of Lent and the other fast days prescribed by Holy Mother Church, she observed two other Lents during the year and took only bread and water on the vigils of the feasts of the Blessed Virgin Mary. Here we must observe, though St. Rita mortified herself most rigorously, she did it so judiciously that her husband and the other members of her household scarcely observed it. God wrought in her the same miracle He wrought in favor of the Hebrew youths at the court of Babylon, who grew more beautiful because they fasted and abstained; for the more St. Rita fasted and punished her body by penance, the more beautiful and graceful she became. But though everyone admired the marvellous beauty and grace of St. Rita, she was more admired for the beauty of her soul which was well known to every one in Rocca Porrena, by reason of her edifying life, and on account of the numberless good works she performed.

In her intercourse with her neighbors, St. Rita was most affable, and in her conversations she never uttered a word that could in any way offend. And when she heard any one speak ill of a neighbor, she reproved mildly the speaker, either by defending the character of the absent one, or artfully changing the subject of conversation. Many and many were the persons who came to her for advice and consolation in their trials and troubles, and no one ever regretted their coming. And when any of the wives of the neighborhood complained to her of the cruelty of their husbands, she, who had suffered many years of cruelty, was accustomed, like another Monica, to say to them: *Lay the blame rather on yourselves and your tongues.*

St. Rita was also an Apostle of true charity. As every virtue is weighed by the scales of charity which gives to it the gold of worth and merit, we find in the heart of St. Rita, a rich mine of charity towards God and towards her neighbor. Of her love for God there can be no doubt. St. Rita was all love, the love of God consumed her and for love of God, there was nothing she could do for her neighbor that she did not do. She visited the sick, nursed them and prepared their medicines. She distributed bread and clothing among the needy poor, and, on one occasion, in imitation of St. Martin of Tours, she gave half of her cloak to a poor person whom she met on the street, half-naked and trembling with the cold. In a few words, we may say, that no poor person in Rocca Porrena wanted anything if it were known to St. Rita.

Besides practicing the corporal works of mercy, St. Rita, like a true Apostle, employed much of her time in caring for the spiritual wants of her neighbors. She approached those whom she knew to be careless in the performance of their religious duties, and persuaded them to mend their ways and become fervent Christians. In her frequent visits to the sick, she consoled them with soothing and holy words; exhorted them to patience and resignation; and it is among the traditions of Rocca Porrena, that St. Rita restored many sick persons to health, by reciting one single "Hail Mary" by their bedsides. The disconsolate and the afflicted came also under the care of her apostolic zeal, and her advice to all whom she consoled and comforted was ever the same: "Place all the weight of your trials and tribulations on the shoulders of Jesus Christ. He will carry them for you. Remember He once carried a heavy cross." And finally, St. Rita dissolved enmities and hatred that existed among her neighbors, as did her father and mother when they were the Peace-makers of Rocca Porrena. Her earnest words of burning zeal penetrated wrathful hearts, quenched the blazing fires of hatred and revenge, and made enemies kiss and embrace.

Her numerous acts of charity, or the time spent in visiting the sick and the poor, did not, in the least, interfere with the care or government of her household, nor with her own private devotions. Besides saying the morning and night prayers which she had learned at the knees of her pious mother Amata, St. Rita meditated every day on the principal mysteries of our holy faith, but her favorite meditation was the Passion of Jesus Christ. Many times while meditating this great mystery, she would fall into a trance, and on recovering her senses, it would seem as if she had been suffering a mysterious martyrdom in the interior of her soul. She also was very devout to Jesus in the Blessed Sacrament, and made as many visits as possible to her parish-church. For she dearly loved to be near that fire of divine love, and never wished to leave it. Finally that she might have protectors on earth, as well as powerful advocates in heaven, she was a devout servant of the Blessed Virgin Mary, and a fervent client of St. John the Baptist, St. Augustine and St. Nicholas of Tolentine. Truly may we say, without detracting from the many women who are now saints in heaven, there is none more glorious than Sister St. Rita of Cascia.

CHAPTER XI.

Death of Ferdinando—Sorrow of St. Rita

ST. RITA, before and especially after her marriage, had made a honey-comb of her heart, so to speak, filled with the odor and sweetness of virtues. Each virtue represented, as it were, a beautiful and fragrant flower, bound together by the girdle or cincture of charity, and formed the most exquisite bouquet she could offer to her divine Lord after she had calmed the boisterous winds that had howled threateningly around her, during the time her husband was an easy prey to the ungovernable impulses of his violent passions. But alas, the days of harmony and peace were soon to be followed by a tragedy that was to cause grief and sorrow in the heart of St. Rita.

Though St. Rita had reformed her husband and had also made him a man of peace, Ferdinando had not a few enemies in Rocca Porrena. Before his marriage, and for some years after, he had engaged in many disputes and contentions with companions as hot-headed and impulsive as himself, but as he was ready and adept with the stiletto or dagger, he was generaly the victor over his adversaries. These persons became Ferdinando's enemies; a poisonous hatred rankled in their breasts, and though he avoided their company, they sought the occasion to avenge themselves. His enemies, not daring to encounter him singly, banded together, as cowards generally do, and meeting him, one day, outside of the walls of Rocca Porrena, attacked him, stabbed him to death, and left his lifeless body, lying by the roadside, bleeding from a dozen wounds.

Some historians say that Ferdinando was not murdered in cold blood, as the saying is. They claim that he himself, in a fit of anger, provoked the quarrel and even struck the first blow of the altercation in which he lost his life. Others say that the violent death of Ferdinando was a visitation from God, in punishment for his extreme cruelty to St. Rita during the early age of his marriage, but that we may piously believe, though he did not have the sweet consolation of receiving the last Sacraments, that God had mercy on his soul, on account of the ocean of merits which his holy wife had treasured in heaven.

When the news of the death of Ferdinando and all the circumstances connected with it reached the ears of St. Rita, she was thrown into a paroxysm of grief. She wept as if her heart were breaking, and though her friends and kind neighbors tried, as best they could, to console her, she would not be consoled. Naturally, St. Rita felt, as every good and holy wife must feel, the sudden taking away of her husband. But what grieved her heart and soul most was that he passed from this life to the other without being fortified with that viaticum, which gives the dying Christian the happy assurance of a safe journey from time to eternity. In her grief and sorrow, St. Rita prayed to God from the altar of her heart and said to Him: "O God, enter not into judgment with thy servant Ferdinando, for in thy sight no one will be justified." She also prayed to Jesus, her divine Lord and Master, the Judge of the living and the dead, and implored Him to grant that His precious Blood, shed for the redemption of mankind, was not shed in vain for the soul of her husband, Ferdinando. And out from the grief-laden heart of that sorrowful widow came so loud and plaintive a cry for the pardon of her husband's faults and failings, that the cry must have been heard in heaven, and, as it penetrated the bowels of God's love, it moved Him to mercy. Nor did St. Rita, in the Gethsemane of her grief and sorrow, forget to have recourse to the Blessed Virgin, the mother of the seven Dolors, the sweet Comfortress of the afflicted, to whom, according to the great St. Bernard, no one ever has recourse in vain.

When the dead and bleeding body of her husband was brought home, St. Rita, with more reason than the Patriarch Jacob who looked upon the blood-stained tunic of his beloved son Joseph, again gave full vent to her grief and sorrow, with sobs and sighs, followed by a torrent of tears. And then, all of a sudden, as if a whisper from heaven had reached her ears, in the twinkling of an eye, her sobs and sighs lost their voices, the fountains of her tears became dry, and, arming herself with a resignation like to that of Jacob, her heart and soul praised the name of the Lord, who was pleased to take to Himself the husband whom He had given her at the foot of His altar. O strong and valiant woman, where can we find your equal! To what can we compare you? You who bore with admirable patience the excessive grief and poignant sorrow which penetrated every fiber of your loving heart as you gazed upon the bleeding remains of him whom the bonds of matrimony had made a part of your life.

Not satisfied with that act of resignation to the will of God, who saw in the crucible of her patience the carats of the gold of her fortitude, she adorned and embellished her resignation with the most precious stone of pardon; for, in imitation of Jesus Christ, who, when dying on the wood of the Cross, asked His heavenly Father to pardon His executioners, so also did St. Rita plead for the murderers of her husband. She herself pardoned them from the bottom of her heart, thus putting into practice that holy doctrine which Jesus Christ taught from the pulpit of the Cross.

After the funeral ceremonies were over, and the mortal remains of her husband were placed in the cemetery of Rocca Porrena, St. Rita continued the exercise of those virtues which she had already been in the habit of practicing, and free from many of the cares of her married life, she determined to live solely for God, the only Lord and Master of her soul.

CHAPTER XII.

St. Rita Makes a Sacrifice of the Lives of Her Two Sons to God

THE DEATH of her husband, Ferdinando, made St. Rita a widow, but she was not left alone. God had blessed her, as we have already observed, with two handsome sons who were now grown up, and on these she centered her utmost care and attention. She daily implored God, with the most fervent prayers, to preserve their innocence, and aid her to guide them in the path of His holy law in which she had instructed them. Giovanni and Paulo, the children of St. Rita, became what their saintly mother moulded them. They grew up God-loving and God-fearing children. They loved their good mother with all the fulness of their boyish hearts, and no boys could be more respectful or obedient to a mother than were Giovanni and Paulo.

As they advanced in years, St. Rita, with the quick perception of a mother, noticed that a change was taking place in the characters of her sons, and that sometimes, not unlike their departed father, they appeared to be sullen, morose and irritable. Especially, did she observe a notable change in Giovanni, who was scarcely sixteen years of age. Young as they were, and even in spite of the religious training they had received from their mother, Giovanni and Paulo had become somewhat imbued with that false idea of honor and justice which made it incumbent on the nearest of kin, to execute vengeance on the slayer of a relative. This criminal and unauthorized right of revenge was much in vogue in Italy, at the time St. Rita lived, and was called: *La Vendetta.*

Though St. Rita had observed, that, from time to time, her sons made remarks relative to the murder of their father, it never entered her mind, that they had any thought of avenging his death. One day, however, from a conversation she overheard between her two sons, she learned, to her great surprise and sorrow, that they were inclined to revenge the assassination of their father.

Like the good and saintly mother she was, St. Rita determined to destroy and stifle so heinous and criminal a desire. Summoning Giovanni and Paulo to her side, she told them what she had heard, and begged them, with tears and supplications, to erase from their minds all desire of revenge, and to forget that their father was assassinated. She also placed before their eyes the example of Christ, who asked pardon for those who had crucified Him and for whom He suffered to give them eternal life. By means of this beautiful example, she sincerely hoped she would be able to persuade her sons to pardon the murderers of their father. She furthermore reminded them, that though they had lost their earthly father, they would gain a heavenly one if they would pardon from their hearts. And finally she represented to them the terrible sin the homicide commits, and plainly told them that they themselves would be murderers, if they avenged the death of their father.

In this manner did St. Rita try to keep and guide her sons in the path of the fear of God. After some time, as we may read in the Decree of her Canonization, when she saw her sons persist in their desire for vengeance, she fled to the crucifix and related the whole affair to Christ, fervently beseeching Him, either to change the desires of her sons, or no longer spare their lives. God heard the prayer of St. Rita. Both her sons died within a year, well prepared to go before the judgment-seat of Almighty God.

O glorious St. Rita! The fame of your sacrifice will never die. The pages of history make mention of no sacrifice more generous than your sacrifice. It is true Abraham was willing to sacrifice his son Isaac, but he was commanded by Almighty God to do so. Your sacrifice was an exact copy of the sacrifice which the Eternal Father made of His only Son on the Cross; for you, not satisfied with pardoning the murderers of your husband, even saved their lives, by offering to God the sacrifice of the lives of your two beloved sons, Giovanni and Paulo.

CHAPTER XIII.

The Penitential Life of St. Rita After the Death of Her Two Sons

ST. RITA was now alone in the world. She was both widow and orphan. The bodies of her husband and two sons were lying, side by side, in the cemetery of Rocca Porrena, and her aged parents, Antonio and Amata had gone to their reward, though we do not know the exact time of their death. Free, therefore, from all the ties that had hitherto bound her to the world, St. Rita resolved to live solely for God, and to spend her time wholly occupied in the service of God. Accordingly, she spent a goodly part of her time in a retired part of the church, praying with ardent devotion and recollection, and never ceased to give thanks to God, for all the graces and favors He had bestowed upon her, during the whole course of her life. And because she hoped that God would lead her, one day, into that other state of life to which she aspired, even from the days of her early girlhood, she again offered herself, body and soul to God, renouncing forever, for the love of God, all the joys and pleasures the world might offer her.

With her heart thus filled with the fire of divine love, one day, St. Rita happened to be in church listening to a sermon. In the course of his preaching, the priest had occasion to quote the words of Christ: *If thou wilt be perfect, go sell what thou hast and give to the poor, and come, follow me.* St. Rita considered these words a special invitation from Jesus Christ, and resolved to obey the divine summons, and put into practice the evangelical counsel, by renouncing all her temporal goods and enter some religious house, wherein she could follow, day by day, her divine Spouse and Master Jesus Christ until the end of her life. From that day forward, St. Rita added new fasts to the many she was already wont to observe, and increased the number and rigor of her penances. She now fasted on the vigils of the feasts of her special patrons, St. John the Baptist, St. Augustine, and St. Nicholas of Tolentine. And she daily solicited their aid and assistance, to help her to fit herself for the religious state to which she aspired. After the death of her husband, she put on a garment of hair-cloth, and repeatedly punished her delicate body with a discipline, and in imitation of the holy widow Judith, she lived a most retired life. So strong and vehement was St. Rita's desire to separate herself from all contact with the world, that she actually, so to speak, turned her house into a holy prison. She closed all the windows of her home, except one near the door, and a little one in the roof, through which she could look up to heaven. She never left her home unless to go to church, or to visit the sick, or to perform works of charity among her poor and needy neighbors. There is near the house in which St. Rita lived, a very high reef, called the Reef of Rocca Porrena. Concerning this reef, it is tradition, that St. Rita climbed, many times, to the topmost part of this reef to be nearer to heaven, and that she spent many hours there in prayer and meditation. Words fail to tell the true story of the penitential and retired life of St. Rita after the death of her two sons. She spent most of her time praying, conversing with her beloved Jesus, asking Him continually to admit her among the virgins who served Him within the sacred and holy walls of the cloister.

Many and many a time did she say to Jesus: "O my dear Lord and Master. Since I am free now, when will the time come, when you will admit me into the haven of religion?" Seeing, however, that her divine Lover did not give a quick response to her prayers, she wept bitterly, thinking that her divine Master would not open to her the doors of the cloister, because there was something wanting in her love and affection towards Him.

In those times of affliction, a few moments meditation on the abandonment of Jesus, by His eternal Father, as He hung dying on the Cross on Calvary, consoled her, and she would say to herself: "My loving Saviour drunk to the very dregs the bitter cup of abandonment, to animate and teach that all who would walk on the sorrowful way of the Cross, must, at least, taste of one drop of His bitter chalice."

Thus consoled, St. Rita would renew her supplications to Jesus, asking Him, again and again, to open to her the doors of the cloister; for St. Rita had made up her mind to continue knocking at the door of the Sacred Heart of Jesus, until she would hear His sweet voice saying to her: "Arise, Rita, make haste my beloved spouse, and come."

CHAPTER XIV.

St. Rita Applies for Admission to the Convent. Her Request is Refused

As we already know, St. Rita was extremely anxious to embrace the religious state of life, and since she had a particular devotion to the great St. Augustine and his spiritual son, St. Nicholas of Tolentine, she desired to become a spiritual daughter of the saint by joining a community of nuns that was governed and guided by the same rule which St. Augustine gave to the community of religious he founded when he was Bishop of Hippo, in Africa. At the time St. Rita lived in Rocca Porrena, there were two communities of Augustinian nuns in Cascia. One community resided in the convent known by the name, St. Mary Magdalen, or the Magdalena; the other was named after St. Lucy, the Martyr. When these convents were founded we do not know, but we do know that in the year of our Lord 1329, the Bishop of Spoleto granted certain privileges to the community of the convent of St. Lucy.

St. Rita knew that in both of those convents the nuns served God to their hearts' content, and burning with those desires which were kindled in her heart when she was but a child, she became more anxious than ever to become a nun and follow the Lamb whithersoever He goeth. Sometimes St. Rita made the journey from Rocca Porrena to Cascia. On those occasions, which, in fact, were pious pilgrimages, her guardian angel always guided her steps into the church attached to the Maddalena convent, where she prayed and meditated until it was time to return home.

One day while she knelt in the little oratory of her house, her eyes fixed on the crucifix, speaking to Jesus and telling Him how anxious she was to enter the cloister and become a nun, a ray of divine consolation penetrated her heart and soul. St. Rita arose from her kneeling posture, and prepared to go to Cascia. Once on the highway, that ray of divine consolation gave haste to her footsteps which brought her direct to the very door of the convent of the Maddalena. With a trembling hand she knocked at the convent door, and in answer to her call, the door was opened by the sister-portress, who, learning that St. Rita desired to speak with the prioress, politely ushered her into the guest-chamber. When the prioress, a sweet-faced venerable nun, came, St. Rita made known, in as few words as possible, the object of her visit.

She told the prioress that from the time she was a child, she had desired to consecrate her virginity to God. That she would have done so had not obedience to her parents prevented her, but being free now, she coveted the Augustinian habit, so that she might better serve the Lord, though she recognized she was unworthy to become a spiritual daughter of the great and glorious St. Augustine. The prioress listened with attention to the humble but earnest petition of St. Rita to be admitted into the community, and kindly told her that she would present her application for membership before a Chapter Meeting of the nuns of the community. We must observe here, that it is a rule of the Augustinian Institute of nuns, not to admit to their communities any but young girls, whose vocations are certain, though widows may also be admitted, but only by special dispensation.

We must, therefore, not be surprised that the nuns of the Maddalena Convent of Cascia, refused to admit St. Rita into their community, and, indeed, a majority of the nuns hinted, that, since no widow had been received into the convent from the time of its foundation, it would be a blot on the Maddalena were they to admit St. Rita as a member of the community, though they knew her to be a person of the most irreproachable character and possessed even of eminent piety and sanctity.

When the prioress of the convent told St. Rita that the nuns had, in public chapter, voted against admitting her as a member of the community, she received the news with a calm exterior, though in her heart she was very much disappointed. Instead of returning to Rocca Porrena, St. Rita remained in Cascia in the house of a friend, and, after a short lapse of time, made a second application only to receive a second refusal. She applied a third time, and most eloquently besought the nuns to admit her into their community, even as a servant, alleging that she did not consider herself a worthy companion of the spouses of Jesus Christ. Her pleading was all in vain, and because God wished to try further the patience of Rita, He permitted the nuns to remain firm in their decision, and thus St. Rita was told for the third time by the prioress that it was *impossible* to admit her as a member of the community, and that she should cease further importunities.

When the door of the Maddalena was closed against

her, St. Rita returned to Rocca Porrena, judging that the time had not yet arrived for her to obtain that happiness to which she aspired. Yet deep down in her heart, she felt that God would soon come to her aid, and, by His omnipotence, help her to overcome what the prioress of the Maddalena Convent has said was *impossible.*

CHAPTER XV.

St. Rita Enters the Maddalena Convent in a Miraculous Manner

WHEN St. Rita returned to Rocca Porrena from Cascia, she began what proved to be her first successful trial against the *impossible.* With the words of the prioress of the Maddalena ringing in her ears: "My dear woman, it is impossible for you to become a member of our community," St. Rita determined to use every holy means to make possible what human lips had told her was impossible. With this determination dominant in her mind, St. Rita spent nearly all her days, and a goodly portion of her nights, supplicating her beloved Jesus to shorten the time of her anxiety, and admit her as one of His brides within the enclosed walls of the cloister. Not content with importuning Jesus with the most fervent prayers and exercises of penance and mortification, St. Rita also implored the aid of her patrons St. John the Baptist, St. Augustine, and St. Nicholas of Tolentine, firmly believing, that through their powerful intercession, God woud hasten the fulfillment of the only desire her heart sought in this world. St. Rita was not disappointed in her confidence and hope, and she, who preferred to be the lowliest among the brides of Christ than to be the most honored of the highest ones of the earth, was soon to taste that happiness she had sought, from the time she was but a little girl. Yea, the time had come, when St. Rita was to make her entrance into the cloister in a most miraculous manner.

One night while engaged in prayer and meditation, she heard a loud knock at the door of her house and a voice which called: "Rita! Rita!" As the hour was late, naturally, a slight feeling of fear overcame her for a moment, but a whispered prayer to heaven gave her the courage to approach the window, which she opened and glanced out to ascertain who called her. Seeing no one at the door, St. Rita thought that what she heard might have been an illusion or perhaps a ruse of the Evil one to divert her from her prayers. Signing herself with the sign of the Cross she resumed her prayers with a redoubled fervor. Again she was interrupted in her prayers by the same voice which said: "Rita! Rita! Fear not. God will admit you into the cloister as His spouse."

This time St. Rita understood the true meaning of the double call that had fallen on her overjoyed ears, and, inflamed by the fire of divine love, her heart gave itself up to so fervent a prayer, that she became wrapped in ecstasy and saw in a vision the three saints whom God had sent to aid her. They were St. John the Baptist, St. Augustine and St. Nicholas of Tolentine. And scarcely had they given her to understand, that the cup of her heart's desire was to be filled to overflowing, than she heard a celestial voice, the voice of her Jesus, who called and said to her: "Come, Rita, my beloved. It is now time for you to enter the Maddalena Convent whose door was so often closed against you."

Awakening, as it were, from a profound sleep, St.

Rita arose from the *prie-dieu* on which she had been kneeling, went to the window and saw a person of venerable mien and aspect standing at the door. He wore a garment of camel's hair, cinctured with a leather girdle and he made signs that she should follow him. St. Rita, recognizing that the person, who beckoned her to follow him, was no other than her patron St. John the Baptist, whom she had seen in the vision, left her house at once, and, with her heart filled with spiritual joy and gladness, she followed her holy guide. They climbed together the rugged steeps of the reef called *Schioppo,* on whose skirt Rocca Porrena is situated. When she had arrived at the summit of the reef, there appeared to her St. Augustine and St. Nicholas of Tolentine, and she felt as if she were standing, so to speak, on Mt. Thabor, so refulgent was the light which radiated from the countenances of her three patrons. Dazzled by the spectacle, St. Rita prostrated herself at their feet, and thanked them, with humble and devout reverence, for all the favors they had obtained for her, and again she recommended herself to their protection.

They commanded her to arise and follow them. She obeyed immediately and walked behind them as they directed their steps in the direction of Cascia. Every step she took told St. Rita that she was drawing nearer and nearer to the long desired goal, and her heart was filled with indescribable joy, as she listened to the heavenly words of her guides as they conversed with one another on the way. It was indeed a memorable journey, and St. Rita must have felt as did the two pilgrims who conversed with Christ on the road to Emmaus; for when she arrived at Cascia, yea, even at the very door of the Maddalena Convent, the desire of consecrating herself, body and soul to her beloved Jesus, was more ardent than ever.

Finding, as was natural, the door and the windows of the Maddalena closed tightly, her guides, nevertheless, led her into the cloister, and then addressed her these words: "Rita, remain a rational bee in the garden of the Spouse whom you have so long and ardently loved; so that, collecting the flowers of virtues, you may build a sweet honey-comb. You are now in the house of your Spouse, Jesus. Love Him with all your heart and soul and your eternal salvation is secure. Return thanks to God for so great a favor done in your behalf. Praise His infinite mercy, and publish that there is nothing impossible to God. Rita the *impossible* is overcome in your behalf." Having said these words, the three saints disappeared. St. Rita, overcome with happiness because she was now within the cloister, spent the remainder of the night in giving thanks to the Lord for the singular favor He had bestowed upon her.

When the morning was come, and the nuns of the Maddalena discovered that a secular was within the cloister, they were both surprised and astonished. Who is she? How did she get in? ran from lip to lip, as, with wondering eyes the nuns fixed their gaze on St. Rita. Some of the nuns began to suspect that one of the community had secretly allowed her to enter the cloister, while others thought that, perhaps, through negligence the door of the convent had been left unlocked. However, when some of the surprise that attended the discovery of St. Rita in the cloister had passed away, the nuns, in a body, approached her and asked: What manner of person she was, and by what means she had entered their cloister?

St. Rita, with humility written in her gladsome eyes,

and with humility guiding the sweet and convincing eloquence of her eager lips, thus answered them: "I am that poor widow of Rocca Porrena who many times asked to be admitted as a member of your community, and was as many times refused as unworthy of so great a happiness. But know, beloved superioress and sisters, that God, wishing to do me a singular favor, sent, last night, to my house in Rocca Porrena, His precursor, St. John the Baptist, accompanied by that Sun of Heaven, St. Augustine, and that Star of Heaven, St. Nicholas of Tolentine, to conduct me into your midst. Nevertheless, I ask you, in the name of that God who has favored me with His mercy, to accept me as a member of your community."

The nuns of the Maddalena listened with amazement while St. Rita related how she had been conducted into the cloister, and when she had concluded her story, all the nuns, with one voice, cried out, that they accepted her as a companion, and then humbly besought her pardon, for having refused, so many times, her request for admission into their convent home.

CHAPTER XVI.

St. Rita Distributes Her Temporal Goods Among the Poor, and Receives the Augustinian Habit

GREAT indeed was the joy that filled the heart and soul of St. Rita, when the nuns of the Maddalena proclaimed unanimously, that they would gladly accept her as a companion and admit her into their community. And not unmindful of the command of her divine Spouse when He said: "Hearken, O daughter, and see, and incline thy ear: and forget thy people and thy Father's house, and the king shall greatly desire thy beauty," before receiving the religious habit, she returned to Rocca Porrena, to sell whatever property she possessed and distribute the proceeds amongst the poor and needy, so that she might not have a single tie or obligation that would bind her to the world. She lost no time in putting into execution the evangelical counsel; she sold everything she had in the world, to be able to follow, without hindrance, her crucified Lord. Yes, she even did more. She renounced her native village, for she is called, not St. Rita of Rocca Porrena, but rather St. Rita of Cascia.

Returning to Cascia, she repaired at once to hear Mass in the Church which is today the reliquary of her body. While there she heard a sermon on the words of

Christ: *I am the way, and the truth and the life.* These words made a deep impression on her mind, and though St. Rita was an unlettered woman, an interior divine light made her understand the real and true meaning of the text. After meditating for some time on the security of that sacred *way,* on the infallibility of that divine *truth,* and on the eternity of that happy *life,* her heart became filled with a burning desire to walk henceforth on no other way, to seek no other truth, to aspire to no other life. For she said to herself: "I know my beloved Jesus is the way, and the truth and the life." Consumed, therefore, with the most ardent desire of following her divine Spouse, St. Rita received the Augustinian habit in the Convent of the Maddalena at Cascia, and took the name of Rita di Antonio, as may be learned from the archives of the Maddalena Convent.

St. Rita was now in the home of her long coveted desires, she was now on the way to become a bride of Christ, and a spiritual daughter of her beloved protector, St. Augustine, and a spiritual sister of her other protector, St. Nicholas of Tolentine. She, therefore, began her novitiate with so much joy and consolation of soul, that all the nuns were both charmed and edified with their new companion, and thanked God, for having placed in their midst, such a marvellous model of every virtue. From the very first day of her novitiate, St. Rita began to live according to both the letter and the spirit of the convent rules and exercises. And, in order that she might bring herself and make herself nearer and more acceptable to her beloved Jesus, she began the practice of humility both in word and deed. Her progress in this beautiful virtue was surprisingly rapid, and she was a novice but a short time, when she had learned to consider herself far beneath the other religious, and she was often heard to say: "I am not worthy to be the servant of so many faithful servants of Christ."

Her heart was now stripped of earthly affection and not a day passed that St. Rita did not offer it to her divine Spouse, earnestly imploring Him to imprint His image in her heart, as a pledge that He had espoused her. Thus, on one occasion, when she was asked why she was so compassionate to the poor, St. Rita answered in an humble manner: "I love the poor of Jesus, on account of Jesus, because I have the image of Jesus stamped in my heart." On an other occasion, when St. Rita was assailed by Satan, who tried to persuade her that she could save her soul by returning to the world, as well as if she remained in the convent, she put the infernal enemy to flight by simply saying to him: "Be gone, Satan. I belong to Jesus Christ. I have no will of my own. My will is that of my beloved Spouse, whose image is imprinted in my heart." Thus St. Rita, who had chosen Jesus Christ for her Lord and Master, not only surrendered to Him her body, her soul and all her worldly possession, but also her own sweet will; so that Jesus Christ became, as it were, the motor power of all her thoughts and actions. Such perfect resignation to the will of God, on the part of the novice Rita, did not pass unnoticed by the nuns of the Maddalena, who could not help observing that she was a model novice, and, indeed many of the nuns, who had grown old in the cloister, did not look on St. Rita as a novice, but considered her rather a religious who had already attained the height of perfection.

Especially, was the prioress, she who but a short time before had told St. Rita that it was impossible for her to become a member of the community, edified by the religious conduct of the novice. And, one day, after she had spoken, with some length, on the yoke of the religious state, as exemplified in the observance of the rule, in the roughness and poverty of the clothing, in the abstinence from food, and in the continuous exercise of mortification, the superioress felt as if she were listening to the voice of an angel when St. Rita said: "Reverend superioress, as soon as I am instructed by my superiors, and as soon as the ark of religion is placed on my shoulders, I shall shut my eyes, so as not to miss the way. For I know I shall walk securely and safely on the straight way of my sweet Jesus, as did the kine that carried the ark of the Lord when it was restored by the Philistines."

Guided, therefore, by the will of her divine Lover, St. Rita was a model novice. She willingly and cheerfully performed the most laborious occupations of the convent, and was never happier than when she was employed in some lowly office. She was prompt and punctual at all the community exercises, and the sound of the bell that called the nuns to chapel, was for St. Rita the voice of God. In the Community Parlor, where the nuns assembled to pass their time in innocent recreation, St. Rita showed by her joyful countenance, how much she enjoyed the pious conversation of her companions; and when she herself spoke, her words possessed a mysterious power which inclined the souls of her hearers to God.

Thus, with her heart in God, and her eyes always fixed on God, St. Rita found, during the time of her noviceship, the yoke of the religious life so sweet, that she never ceased to thank God for His unspeakable goodness, in having conducted her into the cloister to be a companion of His chosen brides. And as a memorial of her gratitude to God, St. Rita solemnized every year the anniversary of her entrance as a novice into the Maddalena Convent.

CHAPTER XVII.

St. Rita Makes Her Solemn Profession—She is Favored With a Mysterious Vision

AT LAST the time came for which St. Rita sighed so long. She had completed her novitiate, and the happy day was come, on which she was to make the solemn profession of the three vows of obedience, poverty and chastity, according to the rule of the great and illustrious St. Augustine. She made her profession in the chapel of the Maddalena, in the presence of the nuns, and thus became the spouse of the Son of God. Her profession filled St. Rita's heart and soul with unspeakable joy and gladness. She gave herself wholly to Jesus and Jesus became wholly hers. And to make her understand, that the sacrifice she had made was pleasing to God, she was favored with a mysterious vision that delighted her heart and inflamed her soul with the ardent desire to arrive at the pinnacle of religious perfection, by means of the three vows she had made, aided by the virtues which she had begun to practice from her earliest childhood.

Having made her solemn profession, the new spouse of Christ spent nearly all the day in giving thanks to God, for having accepted her as His bride, when she did not consider herself even worthy to be His slave. And recalling to mind all the great favors God had bestowed upon her, and especially that of sending three saints from heaven to conduct her into the cloister, so that He might make her His bride, St. Rita shed tears of joy, and felt that the plenitude of heaven had descended upon her.

On the night of the day of her espousals with her divine Fiance, through the three vows of religion, St. Rita was the recipient of a singular favor that made her supremely happy and pointed out to her a sure way to arrive at the port of eternal salvation. As she was kneeling before the crucifix in her little cell, she saw in a vision, as the Patriarch Jacob saw in a sleep, a ladder standing upon the earth, and the top thereof touching heaven. Gazing attentively at the ladder, she observed God at the top of the ladder inviting her to ascend, and she also saw angels ascending and descending by it. While contemplating the spectacle, she heard a voice which said to her: "Rita, if you wish to unite yourself to God in heaven, you must climb this ladder." When the vision disappeared, St. Rita felt much consoled and was filled with heavenly transports because she had seen God, though it was only for a brief moment.

St. Rita began, at once, to consider the mystery of the ladder she had seen in the vision, and remembering that they were angels who ascended and descended by it, she came to understand, that she must become like them, if she would follow in their footsteps. Penetrating deeper into the mystery, the very steps of the ladder taught her, that she herself must build, at once, a spiritual ladder, on whose steps, made of virtues, she could ascend to heaven, and enjoy there, for all eternity, the presence and the companionship of God.

St. Rita, therefore, understood the meaning of the

mystery of the vision, and, if as a novice she was perfect, she now began to advance from virtue to virtue, ascending, day after day, higher and higher on the ladder of religious perfection. And fearful lest the wind of vainglory should in any way extinguish the light or lustre of her virtues, St. Rita safeguarded them, as carefully as she could, by hiding them from the eyes of public gaze. And considering also that to ascend to heaven by the ladder of perfection, it is necessary to put the foot where first the hand was placed, she judged prudently that to assure the merit of the work of her hands, it was best to hide her works with the steps she took for her advancement in the beautiful virtue of humility. Sister St. Rita understood the true meaning of the words of her divine Bridegroom: "Learn of me, because I am meek and humble of heart."

CHAPTER XVIII.

How St. Rita Observed the Vow of Obedience

THE first resolution St. Rita made, after her solemn profession, was to arrive at the summit of religious perfection, by a strict observance of the vows she professed in the Chapel of the Maddalena Convent. Being closely united to Jesus by the sacred bonds of her vows, she began, at once, to climb the ladder of religious perfection, by placing her feet on the step of obedience, which is, indeed, the first step or rung of the ladder of religious perfection. That obedience is the first step of the ladder of religious perfection, we learn from our holy father St. Augustine who said: "Poverty is a great virtue, because it rules over riches. Chastity is also a great virtue, because it dominates the flesh. But the virtue of obedience is greater than either poverty or chastity, because it rules and restrains the intellect and the will. The Holy Ghost expresses the same truth when He says: "Better is obedience than victims." Hence obedience is more excellent than poverty, or chastity, because the spiritual powers of the soul, which are sacrificed to God, are more excellent than the exterior goods of sensual gratification which are sacrificed by the two other vows.

To understand the nature of obedience, as regards the religious state, we must observe, that there are two kinds or classes of obedience. In the first place, there is an obedience that is called blind obedience. This obedience has no eyes, as it were. It inclines the subject to obey the command of the superior without questioning the command, without taking into consideration the difficulty of obeying the command, or without adverting if the command be unjust or impossible. The expression "Blind obedience" signifies "not an unreasoning or unreasonable submission to authority, but a keen appreciation of the rights of authority, the reasonableness of authority, and blindness only to such selfish or worldly considerations, as would lessen regard for authority." This blind obedience may be called, and is, perfect obedience.

The second kind of obedience has as many eyes, so to speak, as the animals and the wheels of the cart that the Prophet Ezekiel saw in a vision, and the subject who is guided by this obedience understands perfectly the difficulties of the command of his superiors. He feels how repugnant it is to the intellect and the violence it does the will. Yet, notwithstanding this knowledge, he obeys promptly and joyfully, considering easy, even that which is impossible. This kind of obedience is superlative and therefore most perfect.

Jesus Christ, Himself, gave us an example of this obedience. Being divine Wisdom itself, He became obedient even to the death of the Cross though He knew death was repugnant to His divinity. And again when He was suffering a terrible agony in the Garden of Gethsemane, did He not cry out? "Father, if it be possible, let this chalice pass from me;" and then as if recollecting the task that was before Him, He added: "Yet not my will but thine be done."

The angels also practice this kind of obedience, and

though they are pure spirits, endowed with superior knowledge, nevertheless, they not only obey God with diligence and promptitude, but they even make themselves obedient to the welfare of creatures, though they know that creatures are inferior to them in everything. Now since this most perfect obedience, more worthy of reward, because more meritorious than blind obedience, is truly characteristic of the angels, we may call those persons angels or angelic persons, who, on earth, are imitators of the angels in their obedience.

Judged by this standard, St. Rita was, indeed, an angelic woman. So obedient indeed was she, that when commanded by her superioress to do anything, even though she knew the command was impossible, she obeyed with the same promptitude as if the command was easily executed.

It is related by many authors of the life of St. Rita, that the superioress of the Maddalena, in order to put her obedience to a test, commanded the saint to water daily a dead and withered plant in the convent garden. St. Rita obeyed without saying a single word about the uselessness of her labor. She watered the plant every day for a year, though she knew it would not revive without a miracle. God, however, rewarded the obedience of St. Rita; to the great astonishment of the nuns, the dead plant revived, put forth leaves and flowers, and was the most beautiful of all the plants in the convent garden.

We will cite another beautiful example of the obedience and resignation of St. Rita. Pope Nicholas V had declared the year 1450 a jubilee year, to which were attached many indulgences, that could be gained by those visiting Rome. As some of the nuns had received permission to make the journey, St. Rita prompted by motives of piety and zeal desired to accompany them. She therefore went to the superioress and humbly asked permission to go to Rome with the other nuns, so that she might gain the indulgences of the jubilee. The superioress, looking at the disfigured forehead of St. Rita—of which we shall speak in another chapter—did not, at first, feel inclined to grant the permission. However, after a few moments of consideration, she dismissed St. Rita saying: "Sister Rita, I will permit you to make the journey to Rome, provided the wound on your forehead be healed, when the sisters are ready to start on the journey."

Leaving the presence of the superioress, St. Rita went at once to the chapel to ask her divine Spouse if it were pleasing to Him that she should make the journey to Rome. If so, she supplicated Him to heal the wound on her forehead, but if not, she would resign herself to His holy will and the will of her superioress. God seeing the humble resignation of St. Rita, and knowing the obedient spirit of His humble and devout servant, heard her prayer, and wonderful to relate, the wound was immediately healed, and St. Rita was granted permission to accompany the other sisters to Rome.

So perfect, indeed, was the obedience of St. Rita, that she would have rather died than not obey the least command of her superiors, whom she considered the representatives of God and her guides and directors. She was like the sheep that always hear the voice of the shepherd and follow him. Free from the slavery of her own will, St. Rita was so perfectly united to the will of God, that she had no self-confidence and abandoned herself entirely to God. Hence so Christ-like was the obedience of Sister St. Rita, that her every act and all her acts were agreeable to God; for, having once placed her feet on the first step of the ladder of religious perfection, she ascended higher and higher, and nearer and nearer to God, and became what she truly was, a model of the most perfect obedience.

CHAPTER XIX.

The Evangelical Poverty that St. Rita Professed and Practiced

IN THE last chapter we have seen that St. Rita began her ascent on the ladder of religious perfection, by the strict observance of the vow of obedience. Desirous of ascending higher, she next placed her feet, so to speak, on the second step of the ladder, which step is evangelical poverty. Poverty is so eminent a virtue, that Jesus Christ, Himself, professed it when He was born poor in a cold and wretched stable, and died naked on the Cross, His only belongings were three nails and a crown of thorns. Moreover, in His sermon on the mount, Christ gave poverty the first place among the Beatitudes when He said: "Blessed are the poor in spirit, for theirs is the kingdom of heaven."

As regards St. Rita, who knew well that the excellence of holy poverty consists, not so much in despising riches, as in renouncing the desire of possessing them, she made such rapid progress in the practice of this virtue, that after she had made her vows, she never had the least affection for riches. We have already learned, that before St. Rita began her novitiate in the convent of the Maddalena, she sold all she possessed in the world, and distributed the proceeds among God's poor. Thus, in order to be poor, she renounced everything in the world and of the world, so that she might follow her divine Spouse, Jesus Christ. So filled, indeed, was St. Rita with the desire of belonging entirely to God, and of seeking nothing but the things of God, that, when she made her solemn profession, she consecrated herself without reserve to God. Her heart thus stripped of every affection to temporal things, and so free was her soul from every inclination to worldly interests, that she considered them the enemies of her eternal salvation.

Because St. Rita loved holy poverty so much, she never wore but one habit, the very one she received the day of her entrance into religion. This habit she never laid aside during all the long years she lived in the convent, and when she died, she was buried with the same habit. And even to this day, though centuries have passed since her pure soul ascended to heaven, it serves as her shroud, a splendid monument of her heroic poverty. Many and many a time was she asked by the nuns why she continued to wear such an old and patched habit. St. Rita always answered with humility: "Sisters, I wear this old habit to imitate the poverty of my Spouse, Jesus Christ." She meditated every day on the poverty of Jesus, and many times while at meditation in the chapel, she was heard to cry out: "O my good Jesus, to clothe me, you stripped yourself. To make me rich, you lived and died in extreme poverty."

So penetrated was St. Rita's soul with the spirit of poverty, that she was content to occupy a small room or cell, whose only furniture consisted of a prie-dieu, a hard bench that served as a bed, a stone was her pillow, and the walls of her cell were decorated with a few pictures representing different scenes of our Lord's Passion. There in that little cell St. Rita was supremely happy. And when not engaged in convent labor or community exercises, she was accustomed to spend hours before the Crucifix, saying to her divine Lord and Master: "O my sweet Jesus! why should I, a vile creature, a miserable sinner, seek a better cell than the one I have? Why should I desire comforts or pleasure in food, clothing, or recreation, when I know that you had no place to lay your head, and that you suffered so much for me, naked, wounded and nailed to a cross?"

One particular incident in the life of St. Rita will give you an idea how detached she was from earthly things. On the occasion of her journey to Rome, in company with the other nuns, St. Rita happened to find on the way a gold coin which she threw into the swift waters of a river they had to cross. The nuns were surprised at her act, which they considered, at least, imprudent, and some of them reproved her, saying: "We may stand in need of money before we return to Cascia."

St. Rita, sorry that she had displeased her sisters, responded to their complaint with these words: "Sister, I threw that piece of money into the river, because, though the coin was small and of little weight, to me it seemed very heavy, so heavy, indeed, that I did not have the strength to carry it any longer."

Not only did St. Rita practice evangelical poverty, but she also tried to induce others to practice it by her urgent words. Many times did she say to the nuns:

"My dear sisters: if you wish to have the esteem and confidence of the good and virtuous, have little or no love for temporal riches. Observe strictly your vow of poverty. A nun who wishes to belong entirely to God, must be totally detached from all earthly things."

St. Rita believed as St. Paul did, that all things outside of Jesus, which did not help to gain Jesus, are as filth and uncleanness. She was a perfect model of poverty. She was a true religious and truly poor, and the example of her life in the convent was a sublime hymn, so to speak, in praise and honor of holy poverty. During her long years in the Maddalena Convent, St. Rita was never heard to say: "This is mine," or "that is yours," for, having once put her feet on the step of poverty, the second step of the ladder of religious perfection, she only heard the sweet voice of her beloved Jesus saying to her: "Come, Rita, I am poor, and follow me."

CHAPTER XX.

The Angelic Purity with Which St. Rita Observed the Vow of Chastity

WE HAVE already said that St. Rita was a perfect model of obedience and poverty. We will now say that St. Rita, by a miracle of God's grace, was a perfect model of chastity, for this beautiful virtue as professed and practiced in the religious state, is really a miracle of grace. Nature cannot give it, it is truly a gift of God. True we cannot place St. Rita in the number of those virgins who form an assemblage apart in heaven, still, because she preserved always the virginity of her soul, she was like to the angels in purity.

We know that from her earliest childhood, it was St. Rita's ardent desire to consecrate herself wholly and entirely to God, and that she had the greatest horror of anything which might, in the least, mar the untarnished whiteness of virginal purity. Having embraced the marriage state, not because she wished it, but rather in obedience to the will of God and that of her parents, St. Rita, while living in that state, observed the most perfect conjugal chastity. Even when St. Rita was wife and mother, the desire of embracing the more perfect state of life was ever uppermost in her mind. And when death had bereft her of husband and children, we know how promptly she hastened, and how she succeeded in a miraculous manner, to bury herself, so to speak, in the cloister, to becocme, first, a domestic of God and then a bride of the Son of God. Once within the walls of the cloister, St. Rita became an angelic woman, for she acquired, aided by the grace of God, and the strict observance of the vow of chastity, that purity which is characteristic of the angels.

So jealous, indeed, was St. Rita of the vow of chastity, that she kept a vigilant guard over her senses, curbing them and keeping them away from whatever might be the occasion of offense against her vow. She guarded her eyes, by keeping them always fixed on Jesus; her ears, by listening only to whatever spoke of God; her tongue, by speaking only the language of heaven; and her thoughts and her heart by renewing every day the oblation of herself to God.

The angelic life that St. Rita led in the convent, did not escape the notice of the arch-enemy of souls, and God, who wished that the saint should enhance her fidelity as spouse of His Son, permitted Lucifer to tempt and assail her, sometimes by flattery or pleasing suggestions. But St. Rita was too well schooled in virtue to prove a victim to the wiles of the crafty Lucifer, and just as often as he tried to tempt her to offend against her vow, just as often was he defeated. Indeed, St. Rita seemed to know that her chastity was to be the chief object of Lucifer's attacks, hence to triumph over so powerful an enemy, she directed all her efforts to make her body subject to the spirit.

The means St. Rita used to subjugate her body might be called by those who have no faith, or by those who love the pandering luxury of the world, the extravagance of folly. But to St. Rita it was a sweet folly, the folly of her Spouse, Jesus Christ, who died on the cross. To subjugate her body she punished it with fasting and abstinence. She observed three Lents in the year, fasted the vigils of the feasts of the Blessed Virgin, and all the vigils of the feasts of her particular patrons, St. John the Baptist, St. Augustine and St. Nicholas of Tolentine. She ate but one meal a day, and this meal consisted, for the most part, of bread and water. By weakening her body St. Rita became spiritually stronger, and better able to defend herself against the Evil One, hence she was accustomed to say: "We must not have any pity for our bodies; the more we pander and fondle them, the more rebellious they will become against the spirit."

Guided by this rule, St. Rita punished her body without pity, and whenever she felt the least symptom of rebellion in her body, occasioned by some diabolical temptation against her vow, if it happened to be winter, she would cast herself on the snow-covered ground of the convent garden, and remain there until the temptation ceased; or she would put a finger or foot into the fire, and burn away, so to speak, the temptation. Then lifting her soul to God, St. Rita would meditate on the rigors and eternity of the punishments of hell, and say to herself: "Rita, you cannot suffer, for even a little while, the snow or fire which God has sent from heaven. How then would you be able to suffer the eternal pains of hell? Do you wish to go to live forever with the condemned souls? Certainly not. Then fulfill faithfully the promises you have made to God. Observe your vow, and you will never offend your divine Spoues."

Acting in this manner, and reckoning that the sufferings of this world are not to be compared with the glory to come, St. Rita kept her rebellious flesh in subjection, and was able to overcome every attack of Lucifer against her vow. And aided also by the sign of the cross, and with the sweet names of Jesus and Mary ever on her lips, and fortified by the continual exercise of penance—of which we shall speak in our next chapter—St. Rita preserved the flower of her purity, defended as it was by the thorns of mortification, as the rose preserves its beauty, defended by the thorns which nature gives it for its protection.

For a greater security of her chastity, of which the common enemy of souls was continually trying to rob her, St. Rita, like the holy man Job, made a covenant with her eyes, never to look at, or even think of, anything that might be the occasion of fault against her purity.

Never happier than when she was in the chapel, or in the silence and solitude of her little cell, St. Rita actually disliked to go to the convent parlor to converse with seculars, unless it was to give spiritual advice, or console some afflicted soul. And when she was obliged by necessity or obedience, to go outside the convent, she wore a heavy veil over her face, and if by chance she met a friend or acquaintance on the street who recognized her, she never stopped to speak, it being a common saying with her, "In ordinary conversation with seculars, a nun loses much, and gains little or nothing."

More than once, while conversing with the nuns, did she say to them: "Sisters, be careful where you look, where you go, and with whom you converse. There is always danger in what we see becoming the occasion of offense against God and our vow." Hence Sister St. Rita, by crucifying her flesh, by curbing her senses, and by the grace of God, through Jesus Christ, became a model of religious chastity.

CHAPTER XXI.

Mortifications Practiced by St. Rita After She Became a Nun

WE MAY say with truth, that St. Rita was, from childhood, inclined to practice mortification, but it was after she had completed her novitiate and had taken her vows, that she began to practice, with the zeal of an Apostle, what Christ urged his disciples to do when He said: "If any man will come after me, let him deny himself and take up his cross and follow me." Mindful of the promises she made when she professed obedience, poverty and chastity, and having no object outside of Him to whom she was entirely dedicated, St. Rita denied herself, and took up her cross to follow her divine Spouse, and did follow Him on the way of the cross.

Her progress in perfection was truly surprising and marvellous, and in a short time, she became a model of every virtue and the edification of the nuns of the Maddalena, who looked upon her as a saint. The recipient of many and great favors from the hands of God, though she, in her humility, said she had done nothing for her crucified Spouse, St. Rita gave herself up to a life of rigorous and continual penance and mortification. Besides observing, as we have already noted, three Lents in the year, the fast and abstinence of the days commanded by Holy Mother Church, the vigils of the feasts of the Blessed Virgin and of her special protectors, St. John the Baptist, St. Augustine and St. Nicholas of Tolentine, she fasted on the vigils of other saints to whom she had devotion, and observed also the particular fasts of the Augustinian Order. So strict, indeed, did St. Rita observe these fasts, that she ate only enough to sustain life. She only partook of bread and water at her meals, and never allowed any excuse, no matter how grave, to interfere with the fast and abstinence. Though weakened by her continual fasts, St. Rita never spent a moment in idleness, and when not at prayer, she was engaged in some useful occupation. At times when her strength failed her while at work, she would recline, for a half hour or more, on the bare floor, or on a hard bench, and repose as soundly as if she were reposing on a bed of down. She slept but a few hours each night, the remaining hours she spent in prayer or in doing needle-work for the community. She wore always, next to her body, a rough hair garment interwoven with thorns which very often penetrated her delicate flesh.

Not content with thus punishing her body, St. Rita added another and a more severe exercise of mortification. She scourged herself three times a day, and she herself tells us, that by so doing she became strong spiritually and was always sure of gaining the victory over the attacks of Lucifer. The following incident will tell us why St. Rita took the disciple. One day, while hurrying to her cell, one of the nuns asked her where she was going with such eager haste. St. Rita responded: "Sister, I am going to weaken the strength of the Evil One. I am going to deprive him of his weapons with my discipline."

St. Rita used three disciplines to scourge or punish her body. The first was composed of small chains; the second of leathern thongs; and the third of a number of small ropes. She offered the first scourging for the Holy Souls in Purgatory; the second scourging for the benefactors of the community of the Maddalena Convent; and the third scourging for all those unfortunate souls who were in the state of mortal sin. These scourgings were severe, so severe, indeed, that sometimes the blood flowed from her body. On account of her continual fastings and scourgings, the body of St. Rita became so thin and frail, that the bones were visible beneath her flesh. And yet were you to gaze at her eyes, you would forget her wan and pallid face, for they spoke a silent, yet eloquent language, expressive of the purity and sanctity of the heart of a bride of Christ, and to whom Christ was continually saying: "Thou art all beautiful, my beloved, and there is no stain in thee."

St. Rita had also to suffer much from the violent assaults and the wiles of the devil, who, though always vanquished and defeated, was ever ready to renew his assaults and attacks. Sometimes he hid her disciplines; sometimes he told her that scourging her body would shorten her life; other times he would say to her, that if she would not give up fasting she would soon die; and once he appeared to her, under the form of a large and hideous dragon, to try to frighten her. But St. Rita had no fear of her old enemy, and she put him to flight by making the sign of the Cross, or by pronouncing the holy names of Jesus and Mary.

Thus for more than forty years, St. Rita led a life of penance and mortification, and strange to relate, she was not ill a single day. Her first illness came when her divine Spouse called her to go to live in heaven, and to enjoy with Him forever that glory and honor which she merited by her holy and mortified life in spite of the world, the flesh, and the devil.

CHAPTER XXII.

St. Rita's Admirable Progress in Virtue During Her Religious Life

WHILE living in the world, St. Rita had led a life of virtue and sanctity, but when she left the world to become a bride of Jesus Christ, she added new virtues to the old, and spread everywhere around her that sweetest and most fragrant of odors, which St. Paul calls the odor of Christ. Filled as St. Rita's heart was with love for her heavenly Spouse, it became the productive garden of all kinds of virtues, and though she tried to hide her virtues under the cloak of humility, the more she tried, the more manifest they became. United in spiritual matrimony with Jesus Christ, St. Rita's utmost endeavors were to maintain inviolable fidelity to Jesus Christ. He had called her to be His bride, and, on the day of her solemn profession, had placed on her finger the golden ring of religion, set with the most precious jewels, obedience, poverty and chastity. Wrapped in the folds of the love of Jesus Christ, and knowing that the practice of virtues would make her more and more like Him, who is virtue itself, St. Rita availed herself of every occasion to practice virtue, so that she might please her heavenly Spouse whom she had promised to love and obey. Hence if she were calumniated, she bore the calumny with patience; if she were ill-treated, she suffered the ill-treatment with humility; and if she were insulted, she not only pardoned the insult, but also prayed to God for those who insulted her, without opening her lips to say a word in her own defense. So strict a watch did St. Rita keep over her tongue, and so faithfully did she observe the rule of silence, that she lived apart from all human communication, and spoke only when necessity or the good of her neighbor demanded it. When speaking during recreation time, St. Rita never uttered an idle word, and if, by chance, she heard any of the nuns using words she considered frivolous, she would, at once, change the topic of conversation, and speak with great unction and prudence of the wonderful love of Jesus Christ for His chosen brides, or of the holy rule they were bound by profession to follow and obey. Thus St. Rita said to her sisters in religion what St. Paul said to the Philippians: "Our conversation is in heaven," for she always spoke, not only of those things that incline one to think of heaven, but she also conversed interiorly with the citizens of heaven. And that this interior conversation might suffer little or no interruption, St. Rita was such a lover of silence, that she carried always, in her mouth, a little stone, to prevent the movement of her tongue, so that she could not offend against silence even inadvertently.

Her great humility aided also to help her keep silence, for it prevented her often from engaging in conversation with the nuns when they were assembled in the recreation room. St. Rita was, indeed, humble, and she had so low a conception of her merits, that she looked upon herself as not worthy to be a servant, much less a companion of the other nuns. And to adorn and embellish the rich jewel of her profound humility, she took the greatest care to conceal, as adroitly as she could, the singular graces and favors God bestowed upon her, lest vanity would destroy their merits, or human praise or honors would make her proud. But the more the humility of St. Rita sought to hide the splendor of her virtues the more they shone in the house of God for the benefit of the people. For having placed St. Rita, so to speak, in the candelabra of His Church to shine in them, as the splendor of her virtues shone in heaven, God was pleased to make manifest her virtues and sanctity to the entire world, so that all who stood in need of spiritual succor, as well as aid and assistance in temporal difficulties, might have recourse to her powerful intercession.

The fame of St. Rita's virtues and sanctity having gone outside the Convent of the Maddalena, and even beyond the limits of the province of Umbria, multitudes came to Cascia to seek advice and the aid of her prayers. And though she would have preferred to remain in the solitude of her convent cell, than to engage in human conversation, or have any intercourse with seculars, her great zeal in the service of God, and her charity towards her neighbor prompted her to meet and receive every class and condition of peoples. Some sought her prayers for the benefit of their health; some solicited her advice in their temporal affairs; some who had grown indifferent in their faith sought her instruction; and others, with tears in their eyes and on bended knees, urged her to plead with God to deliver them from their sufferings and afflictions. Very few of the very many who had recourse to St. Rita were disappointed. Many sick persons were restored to perfect health. Temporal difficulties were solved through her prudent advice. Enemies were reconciled. Peace was restored in warring families. Scores of indifferent persons were made zealous Christians by her instructions, and many sinners renounced their evil ways and were reconciled to God, after St. Rita had taught them the real value of a sincere act of contrition. There is no doubt, the favors and graces that St. Rita obtained from God for those who sought her aid, were the effects of that wisdom and charity she possessed, for God had endowed her with infused knowledge, and many times when the spiritual welfare of her neighbor demanded it, she spoke eloquently of the mysteries of our holy faith. And blest with that infused knowledge, she excelled, in a heroic degree, in the exercise of the theological virtues, as we are told in the Decree of her Beatification.

The faith St. Rita possessed and practiced was so fervent that, "bringing into captivity every understanding," she was left free to advance in merit. And it was also a lively faith, as was manifest by the numberless good works she performed, and the learned instructions she gave to the ignorant concerning the mysteries of the faith. St. Rita also possessed the virtue of hope in an eminent degree, and this virtue was so deeply rooted in her heart and filled it so much, that we are forced to say that her heart seemed to be too small a sphere for its greatness, for it overflowed, so to speak, to the lips which were constantly telling those who suffered afflictions and tribulations: "Have hope. Trust in God. Forget the things that are behind and stretch forth to those things that are before." St. Rita's charity had no limits but charity. She was all love, the love of God consumed her, and she was continually repeating these words of St. John, words embodied in the rule of the great St. Augustine: "God is charity, and he that abideth in charity, abideth in God, and God in him."

Every work St. Rita performed was done according to the will of her divine Spouse, Jesus Christ. At all times, in season and out of season, she was ready to succor and aid the weak and infirm, the poor and the needy, the afflicted and the sinner, knowing well that whatever she did for her suffering neighbor counted as done for Jesus Christ.

Like all saints, St. Rita had great devotion to Mary, the immaculate Mother of God, whose virtues she tried to imitate, and every time she saw an image of the Mother of God, she was accustomed to say: "What an honor it is to have the Mother of Jesus for my mother."

St. Rita had also great devotion to Jesus in the Blessed Sacrament. And many times, while, in chapel, meditating on that mystery of divine love, she was wrapped in ecstasy. Indeed the Blessed Sacrament became her "Bread of life," and whenever she received our Lord in Holy Communion, for hours afterwards, she experienced such consolation and joy, that she seemed to be no longer in the world, but to be living with Jesus.

CHAPTER XXIII.

St. Rita's Love for Prayer—The Wonderful Efficacy of Her Prayers

BORN out of time, we may say, and really a gift of God to her aged parents in answer to their prayers, St. Rita began to pray in her earliest years. Sitting on the lap of her mother, she learned to pronounce the names of Jesus and Mary, and kneeling at her mother's knees, she learned the "Our Father," the "Hail Mary," and the "Credo" that is the "Apostles' Creed." As St. Rita grew in years, her love for prayer grew more and more ardent, and we can safely say, that every day and many times a day, during the years she remained in the world, the sweet voice of her prayers ascended to heaven, and charmed and captivated the ears and the heart of God.

But prayerful as St. Rita was while in the world, it was when she left the world, that she became the very soul of prayer, and gave herself up to the contemplation and meditation of the divine mysteries of our holy faith. And because she desired to get closer and closer to her divine Spouse, like Mary Magdalen, she spent hours at the feet of Jesus, absorbing the spiritual delights and graces which fell like heavenly dew on her pure and innocent soul. While meditating on the mystery of the Incarnation, astonished at the great humility of

Jesus Christ in becoming man, St. Rita often said to herself: "Why art thou proud, O dust and ashes? Dost thou forget that a God humiliated and annihilated Himself, stooping from heaven to lift you thither?"

The favorite meditation of St. Rita was the Passion of Jesus Christ, and she had so much compassion for the sufferings of her sweet Jesus, that whenever she fixed her gaze on a crucifix, tears came into her eyes. When not otherwise engaged, St. Rita could be found, either in the chapel kneeling before the crucifix, or in her little cell, where, as a memorial of the Passion, she had a few pictures, attached to the wall, representing some scenes of the Sorrowful Way of the Cross.

One of these pictures, as we have told you in another chapter represented Mount Calvary. Fixing her eyes on this picture, St. Rita contemplated all the many torments Jesus Christ had suffered. The heavy Cross He had carried on His torn and mangled shoulders; the jibes, mockeries and insults that had accompanied the stripping of His garments; the extreme pain caused by the nails driven through His hands and feet; and the mental agony of Jesus at the thought, that all He suffered, pierced also the tender and loving heart of His sorrowful and afflicted mother. Continuing her meditation of the other sufferings of Jesus, her heart would become sorrowful, her eyes fountains of tears, while from her lips would come forth sobs and sighs, messengers, so to speak, of the interior pain that she herself was suffering in her compassionate heart.

Another picture, that hung on the walls of St. Rita's cell, represented the Holy Sepulchre where the sacred body of Jesus was placed after it was taken down from the Cross. While gazing at this picture, St. Rita had always the desire to die for the world and to be buried with Jesus Christ in God. Nor could she ever fix her eyes on this picture, without saying: "O most sacred tomb! O holy ark! O celestial temple! that was worthy to receive the sacred body of the Son of God.

It is related of St. Rita, that, on one occasion, while meditating before this picture, she was wrapped in ecstasy, and remained so long unconscious to every one and everything around her, that the nuns, when they discovered her, believed the soul of their holy and beloved companion had gone to a better and a happier life. St. Rita spent a good part of the day, and many hours of the night engaged in contemplation and meditation, and many a time did she feel a little displeased, when the rising sun surprised her at meditation which she had begun at midnight, and she would say: "Why do you come so quickly? Do you wish to deprive me, with your small light, of the delights my soul is enjoying? Let me pray, O sun! Let me meditate. My soul sees more when it contemplates under the shadows of the night, than my eyes do when aided by your splendor."

Besides meditating on the mysteries of our holy faith, St. Rita spent two hours each day petitioning heaven for favors and graces for her own soul and the spiritual and temporal good of her neighbor. She prayed to the Eternal Father and asked Him pardon for her sins, by virtue of that extreme love that prompted Him to deliver up to death His only Son whose death delivered sinners from the death of sin. She prayed to the Son of God, and asked Him to enlighten her understanding, so that her heart might never stray away from Him who is the *way,* and the *truth,* and the *life.* She prayed to the Holy Ghost, whom she considered an ocean of love, and implored Him to cultivate her soul with the dew of His love, so that her heart might become a nursery of both His fruits and His gifts. She also prayed to the Blessed Virgin, and sought some of her super-abundant humility; to the angels for purity; and to all the saints, for a participation in the virtues they practiced in this world. By means of her continual and fervent prayers, St. Rita obtained many singular favors and graces from heaven, not only for herself, but also for her neighbor, for, so efficacious were her prayers, that she obtained from God whatever she asked.

We will cite two remarkable favors that were the results of St. Rita's fervent prayers and powerful intercession. A young child, the daughter of a woman of Cascia, was sick unto death. The attending physician, and another who was called in consultation, confessed that medical science could not save the child's life. The poor mother, overcome with grief, hastened to the Maddalena Convent, and earnestly besought St. Rita to ask God to spare the life of her only child. Moved by pity, St. Rita spoke kindly to the sorrowful mother, and consoled her by saying: "My good woman, have faith. God is good. Your child will not die. You will find her well when you return home." As soon as the woman had left her presence, St. Rita hastened to the chapel, and asked God to spare the life of the dying child. Her prayer was heard and answered immediately, and to the great joy of the afflicted mother, on her return home, she found her young daughter cured of her illness.

The following is another proof of the intercessory power of St. Rita's prayers. On one occasion, there was brought to St. Rita a woman, who, for many years was possessed of an evil spirit that tormented and maltreated her most cruelly. St. Rita lost no time in showing her power over the infernal spirit. Raising her eyes to heaven, she offered a prayer. Then she made the sign of the Cross of the head of the possessed and she was liberated, at once, from the power of the evil tormentor, who, when leaving the body of the woman, uttered a loud and frightful shriek.

The power of St. Rita over the infernal spirits manifested itself many times, and especially while she was engaged in prayer and meditation. Time and again did the devil try to disturb her while she was at meditation, trying to frighten her with loud howls and shrieks, and even appearing to her under the most hideous of forms. But St. Rita feared him not. She always drove him away with the sign of the Cross, and continued her meditation or prayers, as if nothing had happened to disturb her.

St. Rita was also an example of prayer to her holy companions of the Maddalena, and very frequently did she urge them to obey faithfully the command of Jesus Christ: *Watch* and *pray.* Saying to them: "My beloved sisters: since we offend our sweet Jesus, every day, in thought, word, deed and the omission of good works, we should pray every day, and every hour of the day, and weep for our offenses against so kind and loving a Father, Master and Spouse."

CHAPTER XXIV.

St. Rita, Praying Before a Crucifix, Receives a Miraculous Wound on the Forehead

KNOWING that prayer is both a spiritual nourishment of the soul, and a celestial dew that fertilizes and prepares the soul to produce an abundant harvest of virtues, St. Rita became full of ardent desires to taste of this sacred nectar, so that she might satisfy that burning thirst she suffered, when she had become hydropical, so to speak, with the love of her divine Spouse, Jesus Christ. And coveting to drink of the bitter waters of His Passion, like St. Agustine, her spiritual father and ours, St. Rita considered Jesus Christ a sweet honey-comb, distributing sweet and delicious honey to all who seek Him and follow Him on the bitter way of the Cross. She contemplated Jesus Christ, as the Royal Prophet had foretold, encircled by His executioners, who, like bees, surrounded Him, in order that through Him she might partake of the honey of Redemption. She looked upon Jesus Christ, as the miraculous dew that had fallen on the fleece, in the time of Gideon, and considered it a foreshadow of His most Holy Incarnation. And considered, as did St. Chrysologus, that Jesus Christ was tormented on the cross and his side pierced with a lance, so that a copious rain of blood and water might fall upon and sanctify a world of souls. And finally, keeping before her eyes the mysterious ladder she had seen, in a vision, she considered it a figure of the cross raised on Calvary, and actually desired to take upon her shoulders the Cross, so that she might feel, at least some of the torments of the Passion of her crucified Lord. The Lord heard the fervent prayers and anxious desire of St. Rita, and looking with favor on His faithful bride, He deigned to answer her prayers and grant her desire in a most miraculous manner.

On one occasion, there came to Cascia, to preach in the Church of St. Mary, a Franciscan friar, named Blessed James of Mount Brandone. This good father had a great reputation for learning and eloquence, and his words had the power of moving the most hardened hearts. As St. Rita was desirous to hear so celebrated a preacher, she, accompanied by other nuns, went to the said church. The subject of Father James' sermon was the Passion and Death of Jesus Christ. With words, as if they were dictated by heaven, the eloquent Franciscan told the old, old story ever new of the great sufferings of our Lord and Saviour Jesus Christ. But the dominant idea of all the Franciscan said, seemed to be centered in the excessive sufferings caused by the crown of thorns. The words of the preacher penetrated deeply into the soul of St. Rita, they filled her heart to overflowing with sadness, tears were in her eyes, and she wept as if her sympathetic heart would break. When the sermon was over, St. Rita returned to the convent, carrying in her bosom every word Father James had said concerning the crown of thorns. After making a visit to the Blessed Sacrament, St. Rita retired to a small private oratory, in which today her body reposes, and, like the wounded heart, that she was, desirous of drinking of the waters of the Lord to slake the thirst of the sufferings she anxiously coveted, she prostrated herself at the foot of a crucifix, and began to meditate on the pains our Saviour suffered from the crown of thorns which penetrated deeply into His sacred temples. And, with the desire to suffer some of the pain her divine Spouse suffered, she asked Jesus to give her, at least, one of the many thorns of the crown of thorns that tormented His sacred head, saying to Him: "O my God and crucified Lord! O you who were innocent and without sin or crime! O you who have suffered so much for love of me! You have suffered arrest, buffeting, insults, a scourging, a crown of thorns, and finally a cruel death on the Cross. Why do you wish that I, your unworthy servant, who was the cause of your sufferings and your pains, should have no share in your sufferings? Make me, O my sweet Jesus, a participant, if not of all of your Passion, at least of a part of it. Recognizing my indignity and my unworthiness, I do not ask you to imprint on my body, as you did in the hearts of St. Augustine and St. Francis, the wounds that you still preserve as precious rubies in heaven. I do not ask you to stamp your holy Cross as you did in the heart of St. Monica. Nor do I ask you to form in my heart the instruments of your Passion, as you did in the heart of my holy sister St. Clare of Montefalco. I only ask you for one of the seventy-two thorns which pierced your head and caused you so much pain, so that I may feel a part of the pain you felt. O my loving Saviour! Do not refuse me this favor. Do not deny me this grace. I will not leave here consoled, if you send me away without so desired a pledge of your love."

When St. Rita had concluded her prayerful petition, her divine Spouse, not wishing to resist any longer the desire of His faithful bride, granted her request. Making of His crown of thorns, so to speak, a bow, and of one of the thorns, an arrow, Jesus fired it at the forehead of St. Rita with such impetus and force, that it penetrated the flesh and bone, and remained fixed in the middle of the forehead, leaving a wound that lasted all her life, and even to this day, the scar of the wound remains plainly visible. The pain that followed, when the thorn penetrated the forehead of St. Rita, was so acute and intense, that she fell into a swoon, and she would have died, then and there, had not Jesus, who wounded her, preserved her life, so that she might feel, as she had earnestly desired, at least, a part of the pains and torments of His Passion. On recovering herself, and knowing that she had been favored with a signal and precious token, St. Rita returned fervent and heartfelt thanks to her divine Lover and Spouse.

St. Rita left the oratory bearing on her forehead the sacred wound, and on her countenance evident signs of intense suffering. On seeing the wound, the nuns were more than surprised, but they were ignorant of the mystery. St. Rita, however, guardian of the royal secret, and knowing how important it was to conceal the sacrament the Sovereign King had confided to her, hid it in her bosom and revealed it to no one.

The pain caused by the wound, increased day by day, and the wound itself assumed so ugly and revolting an appearance, that St. Rita became an object of nausea to some of the nuns, who could not bear even to look at her. Not wishing to be the cause of the least inconvenience to the nuns, St. Rita remained nearly all the time in her cell engaged in divine contemplation, and glorying, even in the midst of the pains of the wound caused by an arrow of divine love. Sometimes the nuns visited her in her cell, either to bring her some nourishment, or to speak a few words with her, for they all loved her dearly. And as often as they came, they departed edified by her wonderful patience.

But St. Rita was happy, even in the midst of her sufferings, and when she felt that her sufferings were becoming more intense, she said to her divine Spouse: "O loving Jesus, increase my patience according as my sufferings increase." This prayer, like all the prayers of St. Rita, was answered, and so great was her patience amidst all the pain she suffered, that she called the little worms which were generated by the putrid humor of her wound—"her angels"—for they increased her sufferings whenever they moved or fed themselves on her tender and aching flesh, thus giving her new occasions to practice patience and to merit more and more the love and esteem of her divine Spouse, Jesus Christ.

CHAPTER XXV.

St. Rita's Journey to Rome

AS WE have already observed in another chapter, the Sovereign Pontiff, Pope Nicholas V, had proclaimed the year of our Lord 1450, Jubilee year; and knowing that some of the nuns of her convent were preparing to make the journey to the Eternal City, to gain the treasure of indulgences, granted by the Church on such solemn occasions, St. Rita desired also to go to Rome, for, in her great humility, she believed that she stood more in need of the graces of the Jubilee than did her sister nuns. With her heart full of holy desire, St. Rita went to the cell of the superioress, and, prostrating herself at her feet, humbly asked permission to go to Rome with the other nuns. The superioress, gazing at the ugly wound on St. Rita's forehead, judged that she had sufficient reason to refuse St. Rita's request, for she believed that the very sight of the wound would be the cause of scandal to all who might see it, since the wound was on that part of the forehead which could not be covered or concealed. Hence the superioress felt herself justified in withholding her permission if the wound did not heal, and dismissed St. Rita with these words: "Be resigned and consoled. God will accept your good and worthy desire and will reward you." St. Rita heard with profound submission the words of her superioress, and recognizing that the wound, being incurable, would, without doubt, prevent her from going to Rome with her sisters, she hastened, at once, to her divine Spouse, as to the only refuge in all her necessities, and kneeling at His sacred feet spoke to Him, as never before spoke a bride to her bridegroom:

"O my most sweet Jesus, crucified for love of me! You know it has always been my desire to serve you, though, through negligence, I have not served you as I ought. Nor have I loved you as I should, vile creature that I am, and the beneficiary of numberless favors and graces from your generous hands. Notwithstanding my unworthiness, O my sweet Jesus, grant me the request I am about to ask. I desire to go to Rome to enjoy those spiritual gifts and blessings which your Vicar grants to all the faithful with liberal hands during the Jubilee. Do not deprive me of that great treasure which is the price of your most precious Blood and most sacred Passion, a memorial of which you deigned to place on the forehead of your unworthy servant, by means of one of the sharp thorns that penetrated your sacred head. You know with what patience I bear my wound. You know the joy I feel, because I have been wounded by one of the instruments of your Passion. And you know the thanks I give you continually for having deigned to make me a sharer of a small portion of your Passion. I do not dare to implore you to take away my wound so that I may go to Rome. I would, indeed, be ungrateful if I wished to return to you that sacred gift your loving and liberal generosity has given me. I resign my will to your holy will. I wish to conform myself to your sacred desires. Even if you heal my wound, I do not ask you to relieve me of the pains I suffer. I ask you, rather, to permit the pains to remain, so that I may suffer interiorly, though you take away the exterior wound while I will be outside my convent."

The humble request was pleasing to the Lord, and as it was His will that St. Rita should make the pilgrimage to Rome, He healed her wound at once. St. Rita, observing that the wound of her forehead had disappeared, gave thanks to God for so signal a favor, and leaving the oratory, she returned to the cell of the superioress. Words cannot express the surprise and astonishment of the superioress and the nuns, at beholding so sudden a cure, and they confessed that only the medicine of God, applied by the angel Raphael, could have accomplished the healing of such an ugly and loathful a wound. There was now nothing to prevent St. Rita from making the journey to Rome with the other nuns. The superioress granted willingly and gladly the permission, and said kindly to St. Rita: "Sister, human ignorance can never prevail again the divine disposition."

Accordingly, the nuns of the Maddalena started on their journey to Rome, delighted that St. Rita was to be of their number; and though they were provided with some means for the journey, the means were insufficient, hence St. Rita took it upon herself to solicit alms along the way. The holy and humble nun did this, not only because she was a lover of evangelical poverty, but also because she wished to exercise the function of a beggar for the sake of her divine Spouse Jesus Christ. To some of the nuns who did not look with favor at her asking alms of the passersby, she said with humility: "By begging, I am acting in accordance with the state I profess, and I also give my neighbor the occasion of exercising charity and of meriting an eternal reward in heaven."

As a reward for the sincerity with which St. Rita despised earthly riches, God made use of the following incident to enhance her heroic poverty, and her absolute confidence in His providence. One day, when the nuns were actually without a cent to buy food or pay for a lodging place for the night, St. Rita happened to see a gold coin on the roadside as she walked along. Stooping down she picked up the money, and gave thanks to God for the golden gift. But St. Rita, who confided in the providence of God which prompted the alms of the charitable, threw the money into a river. All the nuns were surprised at what she had done. Some of them scolded her, while others even said she had committed a sinful act, considering their needy circumstances, and they added that the money had been sent by God to aid them in their need.

St. Rita, looking at her sisters, raised her eyes to heaven, and falling on the ground, she kissed the earth, and, with the sweet voice of an angel, said: "Hear me, dear sisters. Do not be displeased with me because I threw the money in the river. The truth is this: though the small coin had little weight, to me, it became so heavy, that I did not have the strength to carry it any longer." Then she exhorted them to have confidence and faith in God, assuring them that they would not suffer need of anything on the journey. "Because," said she, "God, who up to the present, has supplied all our needs, will, with the same generous liberality, give us our daily bread, and will even give us what He did not have Himself, a place to lay our heads." All the nuns were greatly consoled and edified by what St. Rita had said, continued their journey in a happy state of mind. And seeing with what charity every one received them, they learned to love poverty as they had never loved it before, and thanked God for all the liberality He had bestowed upon them, through the merits of their holy sister St. Rita.

When St. Rita and the other nuns arrived in Rome, they visited together the station churches prescribed to be visited, and prayed with great devotion and attention to gain the indulgence of the Jubilee. The great devotion and piety manifested by St. Rita, as she went from station to station was very noticeable, not only to her sister nuns, but also to thousands of pilgrims, many of whom cried out in admiration: "That Augustinian nun is an angel on earth."

After having visited the sepulchres of the martyrs and other places of holy interest in the city of St. Peter, St. Rita returned to her convent with the other nuns, who, edified by her singular piety during all the time of the pilgrimage, gave thanks to God for having given them such a holy companion, and for the happiness they felt in returning to their convent. Especially were the poor and afflicted of Cascia rejoiced, and they also thanked God when they heard the glad and good news that their beloved Sister Rita had returned from Rome. Not one of the nuns felt happier than St. Rita did in returning to her beloved Maddalena, and as she stood on the steps of the convent before she entered, a singular joy filled her heart, her pale face became flushed with heavenly gladness as she stepped across the threshold, and, at that very moment, the old wound of her forehead became visible, and she began to suffer intense pains. Naturally the nuns were surprised at seeing the disfigured forehead of St. Rita, but they recognized, with tears in their eyes, that the renewal of the old wound was in reality a gift of God, and that he had healed it so that St. Rita might make the journey to Rome.

Dating from that day St. Rita's life was, so to speak, a *passion.* She suffered continually the most acute and excruciating pains, which were augmented not only by the strong offensive odor that came from the wound, but also by the little worms which dwelt in the wound. St. Rita suffered all with unspeakable patience, and whenever any of the little worms would fall to the floor, she would pick them up with care and replace them in the wound, so that she might suffer more and more, in memory of her thorn-crowned Spouse who had suffered so much for her. St. Rita suffered with much joy the torments the little worms caused, and, one day, being asked what were those little worms that appeared in her wound, she responded with a smile, saying: "They are my little angels." She called them thus because they were instruments for testing her patience, and they reminded her continually of the torment the crown of thorns caused her loving Jesus.

St. Rita had to retire and live again in the solitude of her cell to avoid inconveniencing the other nuns with the sight of her wound. Her solitary life increased the already rich treasure of her merits. She continued her penitential exercises, prayers and meditation, until the time came when she left this vale of tears, after having suffered a continuous martyrdom for fifteen years, as appears from the Process of her Beatification.

CHAPTER XXVI.

St. Rita's Illness and the Signs that Qualify Her Sanctity

FOR FOUR years after her return from Rome, St. Rita suffered more pain from the wound on her forehead than before she made the journey to Rome, so that her life became really a martyrdom. Moved with compassion for her suffering, or pleased with her wonderful patience, the Son of God came from heaven to visit and console her with His divine presence. This divine visit filled the soul of St. Rita with extreme delight and gratification, and her heart was so consumed by the words of her divine Spouse, that, having sunk her understanding in the extreme bliss she enjoyed from gazing on the divine beauty of Jesus, she would have broken the earthly bonds that detained her soul in the prison of her body, to enjoy forever the happiness she saw, were she permitted to do so. St. Rita gazed attentively at her beloved Spouse, who, like a flower from the heavenly paradise, and a lily from the celestial valleys, invited her to satisfy her thirst and fill her heart with delights, by enjoying the sweetness His divine presence cast around her. But recognizing that the ocean of happiness in which she was engulfed was only temporal, and thirsting to enjoy the eternal, she ardently desired to follow her divine

Spouse who disappeared from her view, after He had given her a foretaste of what His chosen ones enjoy in heaven.

After our Lord had disappeared, there remained in the heart of St. Rita so deep a wound that she became so ill with divine love, suffering so violent an attack of fever, that she was obliged to betake herself to her poor and hard bed, whereon she lay, more dead than alive, without anyone knowing the cause of her illness. Thus for four long and weary years, St. Rita suffered the pains of love, in order that the gold of her patience might be refined, and that she might make a new ring, set with the most precious jewels, which she would wear at the celebration of her espousals with her divine Lord, when she made her entrance into the kingdom of His glory. Besides the pains of her illness, she suffered the torments of the wound on her forehead, and these torments were made more poignant by the continual movements of the little worms which had also increased in number. But anxious to suffer more and more, St. Rita bore every pain of her agony with the most admirable patience, and during all the years of her illness, she never uttered a single sigh or word of complaint, but respired rather, in all her actions, the celestial love that was consuming her heart with the flames of the divine fire. Having become ill with divine love, because her beloved Spouse had left her after a short visit, St. Rita experienced a love, strong as death, which, however, did not take away her life but rather spared it, so that she actually suffered the pains and agony of death without dying. However, in the midst of all her afflictions, St. Rita sought no human relief. Her chief delight was to feed her soul and body with the bread that came down from heaven, and to quench her thirst with the bitter chalice of the Passion of her divine Spouse, Jesus Christ. Thus for four years her life was really miraculous, nourished only by the Body and Blood of Jesus Christ.

To show how dear St. Rita was to her divine Spouse, and to make manifest the fact that St. Rita can obtain, even the impossible, from God if she ask it, divine providence disposed her, while she was ill, to ask that a flower and two figs be brought her, from the little garden which St. Rita, at one time, owned and cultivated with her own hands. A garden which could be truly called the inheritance of God, and the garden of her heavenly Spouse, because she had sold it before entering the convent, and had distributed the proceeds amongst His needy poor.

One day, in the month of January, a cousin of St. Rita's came to the Maddalena Convent to visit her. The visit was a short one, for that particular day St. Rita was very ill and suffered much. On taking her leave, her relative asked St. Rita if she could do any favor for her. "Yes, cousin," said the saint; "bring me a rose from the garden of my old home in Rocca Porrena." St. Rita's request surprised her cousin, who thought that perhaps her mind was affected by her illness, and besides, as it was midwinter, and the climate of Rocca Porrena exceeding cold, her relative and the nuns who were in attendance could not be persuaded that the rose could be found. Nevertheless, to humor the saint, her cousin told her that she would try to fulfil the errand, though she thought it would be impossible to find what she asked for. St. Rita responded: "My dear cousin, there is nothing impossible to God." The security with which St. Rita spoke these words, determined her cousin to set out, at once, for Rocca Porrena, and to her great astonishment and amazement, on entering the garden, she saw, on a sapless and leafless rosebush, a beautiful red rose in full bloom. She plucked the rose, and returned to Cascia as quickly as possible and gave the rose to St. Rita. The saint received the rose, with great joy and gladness, and a heavenly smile lighted up her countenance as she kissed it reverently, while her heart gave thanks to God, as she contemplated in that rose her sweet Jesus crowned with thorns. St. Rita then handed the miraculous flower to the superioress, and from her hand it passed into the hands of all the nuns, who, after admiring its marvellous beauty, returned fervent thanks to God, who, to make manifest the sanctity of their beloved sister Rita, had caused a most beautiful rose to grow in the midst of a cold winter. To commemorate this miraculous event, roses are blessed each year in all the churches of the Augustinian Order on the feast of St. Rita and distributed to the faithful.

Shortly after the miracle of the rose, God wrought another miracle at the request of St. Rita. On the occasion of another visit to the convent, in the same month of January, St. Rita asked her cousin to go and bring two figs she would find on a certain frozen fig tree in the garden at Rocca Porrena. This time, without the least doubt in her mind, the woman hastened to bring the figs. She had no difficulty in finding the tree St. Rita had described, and on it were two ripe and luscious figs. With no less joy than admiration, at seeing this second miracle, she picked the figs and brought them to St. Rita. St. Rita received the figs with the greatest joy, and again did the nuns thank and praise God for having qualified, for the second time, the sanctity of their holy and beloved sister. But St. Rita, elevating her spirit to a contemplation of the mysterious, considered the two miracles a warning that the time was near at hand, when she would pass from this life to enjoy for all eternity, the incorruptible flowers and seasoned fruits of the celestial paradise.

CHAPTER XXVII.

St. Rita's Happy Death

ST. RITA knowing that the miracles of the figs and the rose were divine predictions of her coming death, she already seemed to hear the very same words that the divine Bridegroom of the Canticles spoke lovingly to His spouse: "Arise, make haste, my love, my dove, my beautiful one, and come. For winter is now past, the flowers have appeared, and the fig tree hath put forth her green figs. Show me thy face, and let thy voice sound in my ears: for thy voice is sweet, and thy face comely."

St. Rita considered these words as spoken to herself, because from the day she saw the beautiful and marvellous rose and the ripe figs, she was certain that the time was near, when the mortal bonds that bound her to this life would be burst asunder, and she would leave this valley of sorrow and tears, to go to enjoy forever that life and that happiness which she most ardently desired, with her divine Spouse and Master, Jesus Christ.

To make St. Rita sure and certain of her near departure from this world, and to invite her to the joys and delights of the celestial paradise, Jesus Christ, accompanied by His blessed Mother, appeared to St. Rita a short time before her death, and thus said to her: "I am your celestial Spouse, who kindled in your heart the fire of divine love, and filled your soul with virtues, in accordance with your ardent desires. I am now come to tell you glad and joyful news. Rita, within a few days, you will depart from this world, to enjoy an eternal rest in your celestial country."

This visit of Jesus Christ and His most blessed Mother filled St. Rita's heart and soul with a flood of unspeakable joy. She knew now that the winter of her torments and sufferings was at an end, and that the gates of heaven were soon to be opened to receive her. A struggle was now going on between the body and soul of St. Rita. Her body, though weakened and emaciated by fasting and penance, wished to retain the soul; and the soul wished to break the prison bars of the body to be with Christ, to whom St. Rita was already united, so that she could cry out with the Apostle St. Paul: "And I live, now not I—though detained in this valley of tears—but Christ liveth in me." Many and fervent were the heartfelt thanks that St. Rita gave to Jesus for having favored her with His divine presence, nor did she forget to thank the Blessed Virgin Mary, the sweet Mother of her divine Spouse, whom she loved with a most tender and ardent love.

When the nuns of the Maddalena learned that St. Rita had been favored with a vision of Jesus Christ and His most blessed Mother, and that it had been revealed to her that she would soon leave them to be united with her divine Spouse who was their Spouse also, they kneeled around her bed, and gazed, with tearful eyes, on their beloved sister, whose face was radiant with heavenly joy, as she spoke these humble and tender words: "My dear superioress and sisters: The time is at hand when I must go to live with my beloved

Spouse. I may have offended you, by not loving you enough, or by not being at times as obedient as our holy rule prescribes. I ask you to pardon all my faults against charity and obedience. And because I know that I have caused you some inconvenience and annoyance by reason of my prolonged infirmity, and, in particular, on account of the ugly wound that I have borne so long on my forehead, I ask you most humbly to have pity on my frailty, and if I have offended in anything, even involuntarily, pardon my ignorance, and pray to God for me, that your prayers may obtain for my soul that mercy and peace I hope from the divine clemency."

The nuns, hearing the tender words of St. Rita, wept bitterly at the very thought of losing her who had so often consoled them by her very presence, and edified them by her holy example. St. Rita observing that the nuns were filled with sadness, consoled them by saying: "Sisters, I am not afraid to die. I know already what it is to die. It is to close the eyes to the world and open them to God."

St. Rita then asked to receive the last Sacraments, and having confessed, the while shedding abundant tears, she was anointed and received as *viaticum* the Blessed Sacrament of the Eucharist, which calmed, at once, the tempest of pains that she had suffered without intermission, from the time her forehead had been pierced by the sacred thorn. Being consoled by the sacred iris of the divine clemency, St. Rita began to enjoy a total rest from the antecedent torments, and to taste of the eternal delights in the contemplation of the riches and abundance of the home of God. St. Rita was now knocking at the gates of heaven, asking her divine Spouse to open them. She also implored the help of the Queen of heaven, the ever glorious Blessed Virgin

Mary, of the angels, and the intercession of her three powerful protectors, St. John the Baptist, St. Augustine and St. Nicholas of Tolentine. She felt sure that these three saints were waiting to introduce her into the palace of eternal glory, as they had conducted her into the haven of religion.

Realizing that her last hour had come, St. Rita humbly asked the blessing of her superioress, wishing by this last act of submission to enhance the merits of her most perfect obedience. And because she had always loved her sisters in religion with a holy love, her affectionate heart prompted these parting words: "Love God above all things. His goodness being infinite and His beauty without comparison, you should keep always before your minds the great love He has for you as Father, Spouse and Master. Love one another with a reciprocal chaste and holy love. Observe faithfully the rule you have professed, and venerate with a religious affection our great and holy father St. Augustine, who has pointed out to you, by his rule, the royal road to glory. Be obedient to Holy Mother Church, and to your superioress, as you promised when you made your solemn profession."

Having concluded this exhortation, St. Rita blessed the nuns with the last words she was heard to utter on earth: "May God bless you and may you always remain in holy peace and love with your beloved Spouse Jesus Christ." Then, fixing her eyes on the crucifix, St. Rita's soul took flight from this world to an eternal rest in the arms of her divine Bridegroom, Jesus Christ. At the very moment St. Rita expired, one of the nuns saw her soul being borne to heaven by angels.

Sister St. Rita died, during the reign of Pope Callistus III., on the twenty-second day of May, in the year of our Lord 1457. She had reached the mature age of seventy-six years, of which forty-six years she had been an Augustinian nun.

CHAPTER XXVIII.

Singular Events that Followed Immediately the Death of St. Rita

SCARCELY had St. Rita left this world to enjoy the eternal happiness of heaven, than there took place events that prove how precious her death was in the sight of God. Immediately after she expired, her cell was filled and aglow with a supernatural light, and her body sent forth an odor, so sweet and so fragrant, as if it were a mixture of roses, white lilies and other odoriferous flowers. The odor filled the entire convent with a celestial perfume, which doubly compensated for the unbearable odor that had previously come from the wound which disfigured her forehead. The little worms which had, indeed, helped to make the countenance of St. Rita abominable were changed into agreeable and pretty lights which twinkled like little stars, and the wound caused by the thorn shone with the brilliancy of a ruby. Her body had not the sign of a corpse; that body, which before death was almost a skeleton, on account of her continual penances and the four years of illness she suffered, became pliant and soft and fresh, so that she did not appear to be the prey of death, but only sleeping peacefully. She appeared years younger than she was, and her face was more beautiful in death than in life.

As if to celebrate the entrance of St. Rita into the kingdom and home of her divine Spouse, angels moved the inanimate tongues of the bells in the belfries of the holy places in Cascia. At the very moment of her death, the large bell of the Maddalena Convent began to ring out its joyous peals, and when it had ceased, the bell of the church of St. Mary, as well as that of St. Lucy's Convent, were also rung by angels, according to the testimony of Father Donato Donati of Lucca. The pealing of the bells brought a large concourse of people to the church of the Maddalena, and when it was told them, by the chaplain of the convent, that the bells announced both the entrance of St. Rita into heaven, and her departure from this world, the people were silent for a few moments, then their eyes welled with tears and they wept bitterly. They knew and felt that they had lost a mother, and a protector in their labors and afflictions. But bethinking themselves, they were consoled with the thought, that St. Rita would still continue to be their patroness and protectress, if, by their holy and Christian lives, they would merit to retain her patronage.

After the nuns had prepared the body of St. Rita for burial, her funeral shroud being the same habit and headdress she had worn from her entrance into the convent, the body was borne to the church and placed on a catafalque before the main altar. The church was thronged with people, for besides the faithful of Cascia very many came from the neighboring towns and villages. Each one in the church seemed to wish to be first to venerate the body of the saint, and all were astonished and admired the celestial odor her body emitted, and the heavenly lights her countenance radiated, those of the wound on her forehead being the most noticeable, as they shone and glistened with all the brilliancy of the most precious stones.

Of the very many who were in the church, a goodly number had the happiness to kiss or touch the body of the saint, and not a few were recipients of singular favors by reason of this contact. We will mention one remarkable case. A relative of St. Rita had suffered severe pains in one of her arms for many years. Medical science had failed to give her any relief and the arm had become paralyzed and utterly useless. With an ardent faith and confidence in the intercessory power of St. Rita, the afflicted woman approached and touched the dead body of the saint with the paralyzed arm, and the arm was instantly cured of its paralysis to the great surprise of the very many persons who were witnesses of the miracle. Naturally the people broke forth into accents of joy and gladness, and with loud voices praised God and thanked Him, for having given them so signal a proof of the sanctity of His holy servant, and their hearts were filled with veneration for the body of St. Rita, which had now become a most precious relic.

Had it been left to the nuns of the Maddalena, they would have had the funeral services over the body of St. Rita without any pomp or solemnity. But the people of Cascia wished otherwise. Though they knew that the pure and innocent soul of St. Rita did not stand in need of prayers, because she had no sins to atone for, and died the death of the just, nevertheless, because they had lost a mother, a guide and exemplar, they determined that St. Rita's funeral should be conducted with all the pomp and ceremony of the ritual of Holy Mother Church. The generosity of the people of Cascia defrayed the funeral expenses, and never before or since has Cascia witnessed so large a number of people assembled together to pay their last respects to a departed soul. So great was the throng of people that wished to view the remains of St. Rita that the body was left in the church for three days. During these three days many miracles were wrought through the intercession of St. Rita. Many were of the opinion, that the body should not be interred, since it bore no sign of death, but finally all agreed that the body of St. Rita should repose in some place where it could always be seen by those who wished to venerate it.

The nuns of the Maddalena, fearing to lose so precious a treasure, determined to have the body of the saint within the cloister. At that time, perhaps by divine disposition, there was but one carpenter in Cascia, whose name was Francis Barbari. Two of the nuns went to his house for the purpose of asking him to make a coffin for St. Rita's body. On their arrival at his residence, they found him propped up in a chair, so sick and feeble that he could not move a hand or foot. Learning the nuns' mission, a ray of hope penetrated the heart of Francis, and he told the nuns he would make the coffin, provided he were restored to health through the intercession of the saint. As it appears from the Process of St. Rita's Beatification, Francis Barbari was immediately cured through the intercession of the saint, and he had the honor of making the coffin which still contains the body of that holy Augustinian nun, who is the glory and honor of Cascia, and one of the most illustrious saints of the Catholic Church.

When the body of the saint was placed in the coffin, the coffin was brought from the church and deposited in the centre of the oratory, where, as you have been told, St. Rita received the wound on the forehead, while praying before the crucifix. An altar, the first monument to St. Rita, was built over the body of the saint. Around the altar is a low railing. The oratory is separate from both cloister and church, guarded by high gratings of iron, so that the nuns from the cloister, as well as the people in the church, may always see the face of St. Rita, through whose intercession God is daily bestowing graces and blessings on the faithful, especially on the devout clients of Sister St. Rita.

CHAPTER XXIX.

The Worship With Which St. Rita Was Venerated

DEVOTION to St. Rita began immediately after her death. Every day, from early morn until sunset, the church of the Maddalena was crowded with devout worshipers, who vied with one another, in venerating her body, as if she had been already declared a saint by the Church. Not only did the inhabitants of Cascia venerate the holy remains of St. Rita, but even the people of the neighborhood came every year, in processions, on the anniversary of her death, to venerate St. Rita's body, and to give it the honor and homage due only to the body of a saint. Even before the Beatification of St. Rita, the nuns of the Maddalena recited an office of St. Rita on the anniversary of her death, and the convent and the church, both dedicated to St. Mary Magdalen, became known as the church and convent of St. Rita.

So great was the love and veneration of the people of Cascia for St. Rita, that to preserve her memory, they had a magnificent picture painted, by a celebrated artist, for the church. In this beautiful picture are represented, some of the principal incidents of the life of St. Rita. The house, at Rocca Porrena, in which St. Rita was born and lived before she entered the convent, became the object of much veneration, and not many years after the death of the saint it became a church. But though Cascia has the great fortune of possessing the body of the saint, it is the greatest boast, even to the present day, of the people of the little village of Rocca Porrena, that it has the incomparable honor of being the birthplace of the great and glorious St. Rita. And finally the cell of the saint occupied in the convent became, in the eyes of the nuns, a sacred and holy place, where they often entered to pray, and to ask the aid and intercession of their dear departed sister, whom they believed was reigning in heaven with her divine Spouse, Jesus Christ.

As day followed day, the devotion to St. Rita increased, and the miracles wrought through her powerful intercession were multiplied. Cascia became the Mecca, so to speak, of pilgrims from the provinces far beyond the limits of Umbria. The name and fame of St. Rita spread over all Italy, so that the afflicted of every class and condition of life turned their steps, or were brought to Cascia. No one can number the miracles wrought in the church of St. Rita, during the half century of years that followed the death of the saint. Every one of these fifty years brought numbers of persons afflicted with all kinds of maladies to St. Rita's church in Cascia, seeking help and aid from her who seemed to be able to obtain from God whatever she asked. Judging from the many votive offerings presented to the church by those whose prayers were heard and whose petitions were granted, we may conclude that many thousands of the afflicted were consoled, healed, or made happy through the intercession of St. Rita.

Devotion to St. Rita had a very salutary effect on the moral atmosphere of Cascia. Its people became

God-loving and devout Christians. And so great was the love and veneration of the people of Cascia for the saint, that they determined to change the ancient coat of arms, and adopt in its place a figure of St. Rita, holding in one hand a crucifix, and in the other a rose, while her head is crowned with a halo of brilliant lights. This coat of arms was painted on one of the walls of the Council Chamber of the City Hall of Cascia.

That the faithful of Cascia enjoyed, at least, the tacit approbation of the Holy See, to have public worship in honor of St. Rita, even before her solemn Beatification, may be inferred from a letter written by Cardinal Borghese, nephew of Pope Paul V, in response to a letter from the Mayor of Cascia, who sought permission, from the authorities at Rome, to have a large banner made to be carried in the procession held each year in honor of St. Rita. The tenor of the letter is as follows:

My Very Dear Sir:

The Sacred Congregation grants permission to the Community of Cascia, to expend the sum of one hundred and fifty dollars for the purchase of a banner, to be carried in the procession held each year in honor of holy Rita.

Yours sincerely,

CARDINAL BORGHESE.

The banner was accordingly procured. On it was painted a picture of St. Rita and the Arms of Paul V.

CHAPTER XXX.

The Privileges that the Body and Relics of St. Rita Enjoy

THE FIRST and principal privilege, that God has deigned to grant to the body of St. Rita, is that it has never suffered the law of dissolution. It is really wonderful to relate, that though hundreds of years have elapsed since St. Rita died, her body is so well preserved, that there is not visible the least trace of corruption. In fact, St. Rita does not appear to be dead, she has rather the appearance of a person who is sleeping soundly. Her flesh is milk-white; her mouth is slightly parted, so that one may see her white teeth. Her eyes are half-opened, though they had remained closed from the time of her death until the day of her solemn Beatification, of which we shall speak in a future chapter.

The second prodigy is that the habit and veil which St. Rita wore from the time she entered the convent until she died and which served for her funeral shroud, are still intact and in good condition. Not less marvelous is the miraculous virtue of her clothing and veil. From time to time the nuns are accustomed to place pieces of linen or woolen cloth on the body of St. Rita. They then cut the cloth into very small pieces, and distribute them among the faithful. Many singular results have been effected by means of these little pieces of cloth that have touched the clothing of St. Rita. In proof of what we say we will mention a few miraculous results.

On the 10th of May, in the year of our Lord 1525, a little boy, son of Giovanni Francisco di Nardo, a native of San Bruto, was suddenly seized with an attack of apoplexy. For three days the child was unable to take food, or open his eyes, or speak. Full of faith and confidence in the intercession of St. Rita, the poor father set out for Cascia, and having visited the tomb of the saint, he obtained a small piece of her tunic. On returning home, he applied the piece of cloth he had received from the nuns to his son's eyes. The little boy opened his eyes at once, he began to talk and was entirely cured of the apoplexy.

On the 27th of April, in the year 1652, a house, belonging to Signora Clara Calderini, wife of Giovanni Polidoro, a resident of Narni, took fire accidentaly. Owing to the scarcity of water, all hope of saving the building was abandoned. The fire, however, was extinguished almost immediately, by throwing into the flames a small piece of woolen cloth which had touched the veil of St. Rita. This fact is attested by the officials of the city or Narni, May 21st of the same year.

The third prodigy is the sweet odor and fragrance that emanate constantly from the body of St. Rita. This sweet odor is at times more noticeable than at others. Sometimes it perfumes the atmosphere beyond the limits of the church, especially when any signal favor is obtained from God through the intercession of St. Rita. On these occasions the nuns ring the large convent bell in thanksgiving to God for showing Himself so wonderful in His humble servant St. Rita. On one particular occasion, the sweet odor and heavenly fragrance coming from the body was so very noticeable that the nuns were most anxious to know the cause. A few days later they learned the reason. A lady, the wife of an eminent physician of Sinigaglia, came to the convent and informed the nuns, that her son, whose life had been despaired of by her husband and other physicians, had been cured through the intercession of St. Rita. In thanksgiving for this great favor, the overjoyed mother had brought a large silver votive offering, to be placed on the tomb of the saint.

The fourth prodigy is that the body of St. Rita appears to be living, from the frequency of elevating itself, so that it touches the network of wires that covers the coffin. This prodigy is especially noticeable on the feast day of the saint, May 22nd, and when the bishop of Spoleto, or the provincial of Umbria, makes his visits to Cascia to venerate the saint's body. It would seem that St. Rita, the model of obedience to her superiors while living, wishes even after death to practice the virtue of obedience.

The fifth prodigy is recognized in the virtue of the little breads, with the figure of St. Rita stamped upon them, that the nuns distribute, on her feast day, or during the year to the pilgrims who come to visit the tomb of the saint to venerate her body. These little breads are carefully made by the nuns and when made are covered with cloths that have touched the body of St. Rita. By the eating of one of these little breads, many persons, grievously ill with fever and other maladies, have been cured. And many rain and hail storms, and even storms at sea, have suddenly ceased by exposing to the air one of these little breads, accompanied by the recitation of an "Our Father" and a "Hail Mary."

The sixth prodigy is manifested in the wonderful healing power of the oil of the lamp that is kept constantly lighted before the tomb of St. Rita. Many remarkable cures have been effected in favor of those, who, having faith and confidence in the intercession of St. Rita, anointed the afflicted parts of their bodies with a few drops of this oil.

In the year 1620, a very good and devout woman, named Coluccia, the wife of Giovanni Andreas, a native of Norcia, came to Cascia accompanied by her young son who was deprived of the use of his hands and feet by reason of paralysis. When Coluccia had come with her crippled son before the tomb of St. Rita, she obtained a small portion of the oil, and after she anointed his helpless hands and feet, she had the extreme joy and happiness of seeing her son cured instantly. Ever afterwards the young boy was accustomed to say: "I am a child of St. Rita of Cascia."

A like favor was obtained by Alessandro Alessandrini, a native of Amatrice, of the province of Abruzzi, not far from the confines of Cascia. He was at the very door of death, by reason of a deep wound he had received in the thigh. The wound was healed by one application of the oil, without leaving the least sign of a scar.

No less fortunate was the lot of Granicia, the daughter of Antonio Vanatteli, a native of Atri, a village of Cascia. This young girl suffered acute pains, caused by a tumor in her right side. She had recourse to the aid of St. Rita, and by applying the oil to her side, the pains ceased, and the tumor disappeared.

In the year 1616, Pompeo Benenato, a native of Cascia, and governor that year of Ferrara, bled from the nose so copiously, that he became very weak from the loss of blood. Do what they would the efforts of physicians could not stay the flow of blood. Being a man of faith, the governor made a novena to St. Rita. On the last day of the novena, the blood flowed more copious than ever, but on anointing the extremity of the nose and nostrils with the oil, and by making the sign of the cross, invoking at the same time the aid of St. Rita, the flow of blood stopped suddenly. In thanksgiving for this great favor, the governor presented a beautiful and costly lamp to the shrine of St. Rita.

But among the many prodigies, by which God has made manifest the sanctity of His holy servant St. Rita, there is none more worthy of our admiration than the little swarm of bees, commonly called "St. Rita's Bees." We have already seen that a swarm of white bees appeared and hovered around the cradle of the saint, but the bees of which we now speak are those which first appeared when the saint entered the convent, where they now live in a retired place in the convent wall. They leave the convent every Holy Week and remain abroad until the feast of St. Rita. Often times, during the year, they fly through the convent and in the garden, but it is very noticeable, that they first fly to the room of the prioress, as if to ask permission to take their recreation. Another noticeable fact about them is this; they are the constant companions of the nuns while they are kneading the dough to make the little breads of St. Rita, and it would seem as if the little winged-creatures were urging on the work of the nuns by their continual humming and buzzing.

CHAPTER XXXI.

Miracles That God Wrought Through the Intercession of St. Rita After Her Death

IN EVERY age, there have been holy and saintly persons who have verified the saying of the Holy Ghost: "God is wonderful in His saints." The pages of church history are replete with names of saints whom God has honored by making them the instruments of His power, and by communicating to them the gift of working miracles in His name and for His honor and glory.

Among the many and the great saints to whom God has given the power of miracles, there is none more favored with this heavenly gift than the humble Augustinian nun, Sister St. Rita of Cascia. In fact, so marvelous have been the miracles wrought through her powerful intercession, that she has merited the singular and glorious title: "Saint of the Impossible."

Were we to relate the long list of miracles wrought through the intercession of St. Rita, we would be obliged to make the story of her life too long. We will only mention a few of the many miracles brought to notice during the Process for her Beatification.

That God gave St. Rita power and dominion over the common enemy of mankind, is evident from the number of persons she liberated from the tyranny and slavery of the Evil One who afflicted their bodies in various and violent ways.

We will relate two striking facts in proof of St. Rita's power over the Evil One. Perna, the daughter of Giovanni and Elena Tuzi, both natives of Norcia, had been, for many years, tormented by an evil spirit that had taken possession of her body. On the 10th of June, in the year 1491, Perna came to Cascia, and while kneeling in prayer before the body of St. Rita, the evil spirit was forced to leave and go out of her body.

Another woman, whose name was Casandra, a resident of Aquila, became possessed of a devil, God permitting it, in punishment for breaking her promise to go and venerate the body of St. Rita, through whose intercession her sick boy had been cured when he was at the point of death. For the space of three years the devil tormented her in a most cruel manner. One day the evil spirit told her that he would never abandon, nor cease to torment her, unless she went to visit the tomb of St. Rita in Cascia. By force, two of her grownup sons brought her before the body of St. Rita, and Casandra was liberated, at once, from the power of the devil, who, on leaving the woman's body, proclaimed the details of the miracle. This miracle took place in the year 1541.

St. Rita's power in curing the blind was no less marvellous. A woman, whose name was Lucia di Santi, a native of the village of Santa Maria, had been deprived of her sight for the period of fifteen years. On the 18th of June, in the year 1457, her blindness was cured, after she had prayed for fifteen consecutive days before the body of St. Rita.

Another woman, blind of an eye, recovered her full

sight through the intercession of St. Rita, in the year 1539.

A similar favor was obtained by Bernardino, son of Tiberio, who accidentally injured one of his eyes. According to reputable physicians, he was in danger of losing the sight of his other eye. But when he was led before the body of St. Rita, he humbly asked her aid and his eye was healed.

St. Rita also extended her patronage to the deaf and mute. In the month of May, in the year of our Lord 1457, Francesca, the daughter of Antonio, a citizen of Fucella, who had been deaf in one ear, for five years, was instantly cured by invoking St. Rita.

In the same month of the same year, Francesca, daughter of Giovanni di Chiodo, a native of Viseli, a little village of Norcia, who had been mute from her birth, received the power of speech while praying before the body of St. Rita, and caused great surprise and admiration to those kneeling around her, by reciting, in a loud voice, the "Hail Mary." The words of the "Hail Mary" were the first Francesca had ever articulated.

On the 13th of July, in the year 1457, Francesco, the son of Antonio Pasquale who lived in the village of San Cipriano, in Amatrice, who was mute from his birth, began to speak after praying the greater part of two days before the tomb of St. Rita.

Mattea di Cesare, a native of Rocca Indulsi, a village of Norcia, who had been born deaf and dumb, was cured of both her afflictions while praying before the body of St. Rita.

And in the year 1558, Porcia, the daughter of Gerolamo di Angelo, who had been born mute, received the power of speech, through the intercession of St. Rita.

St. Rita is also a special advocate before God for those who suffer infirmities of the throat, as is verified by the following. A certain Francisco di Monteferro was afflicted with a cancer in the throat. As he was a good and devout man, St. Rita appeared to him in his sleep. While in doubt whether the vision were an illusion or not, St. Rita appeared a second time. Francesco told some of his friends of these visions, and asked them if there were any saint with a wound on her forehead. But his friends only laughed and began to make fun of him. St. Rita appeared a third time to him and told him her name. Feeling consoled after this last vision, Francesco went to Cascia and was completely cured of the cancer while he was in prayer before the tomb of the saint. This miracle took place in the year 1510. In thanksgiving to God, for so great a manifestation of His mercy and power through the intercession of St. Rita, the people, who were in the church when the miracle was wrought, formed a procession, and marched through the streets of Cascia. After the procession, a sermon was preached in honor of St. Rita.

A like favor was granted Maestro Francesco of Milano, who also suffered from a cancer in the throat. St. Rita appeared to him three times and told him to go to Cascia to venerate her body, which he did, and was cured in the year 1500.

Giovanna, a native of Fogliano, suffered from a malady of the throat. She could neither eat nor drink and could scarcely breathe. The physician who attended her could do nothing to relieve her. Oftentimes, after being seized with a violent convulsion she would fall into a swoon, and appear as if she were dead. On one occasion, after coming out of a swoon caused by a violent spasm, she said she had seen St. Rita, who touched her throat with her hand and said: "Be not afraid. Arise and spit." Having done as the saint commanded, Giovanna was cured of her malady, the 22nd of May, 1481.

St. Rita was also compassionate towards the paralytics who sought her intercession. Among the many paralytics she cured was a certain woman of Longe. She had been a paralytic for years. Having been brought by some of her family to Cascia, they placed her before the body of St. Rita, and while praying with faith and confidence in the intercession of St. Rita, she was cured. After returning thanks to God and St. Rita, she returned home on foot. This miracle took place in the year 1489.

God also endowed St. Rita with the power to give health to as many of the sick or infirm, who with faith and confidence implored her intercession. Lucrezia, daughter of Notario Paulo, a native of Calforcella, was a victim, for many years, of dropsy. On the 25th of May, in the year of our Lord 1547, while standing in the presence of the body of St. Rita, she was cured of her ailment.

Venucio di Santi, a native of Fogliano, had broken his arm. He promised St. Rita he would make an offering to her shrine in Cascia if she would heal him. His arm was instantly healed. Delaying the fulfillment of his promise, he soon forgot it. One day, while on his way to Norcia where he had some business, a violent pain attacked one of his feet, and it was with great difficulty that he could limp along. Recognizing that God had punished him, for not complying with the promise he had made to St. Rita, with tears in his eyes, he promised a double offering to the saint if she would again cure him, and the pain left his foot at once.

In the year 1539, a son of Loreto di Pietrojaco was cured of the falling sickness, by invoking the intercession of St. Rita.

Ristoro Garrio, a resident of Amatrice, was seized with acute spasmodic pains in the abdomen. He was actually at the point of death, when, by the advice of his wife, he promised to go to Cascia to visit the tomb of St. Rita, and he was instantly cured.

Giovanni Andreas, a little boy of four years, the son of Fabriano Fortunato, happened to fall into a large tub of boiling water. He was injured so much that he could neither see nor speak. His poor mother recommended her little son to St. Rita, and in a few days he recovered his sight and speech.

Cesare, son of Giovanni Francesco Nardo, a native of Cascia, met with a grave accident. For three days, he could neither eat nor drink. His parents brought him to the tomb of St. Rita, and after they and he had prayed for a short time, he was completely cured.

On the 9th of December, in the year 1494, Andrea, son of Giovanni Nucio, a native of Atri, while felling trees, had the misfortune to be struck by a falling oak tree which pinned him to the ground. Seeing that he would be crushed to death, if somebody did not come to his assistance, he invoked the aid of St. Rita from whom he had received a favor. Wonderful to relate, the tree parted, and Andrea escaped without the least injury.

St. Rita also enjoyed the privilege of saving those whose lives were in danger by drowning. On the 1st of May, in the year 1539, Antonia, the daughter of Giovanni Silvestro, a native of Rocca Porrena, fell from a bridge into a river. The current was so swift, that, in a short time, she was carried a little more than a mile, from where she fell into the water. The many persons, who sought her body, believing she was drowned, found her sitting on the bank of the river safe and uninjured. She told them she had been saved from drowning by St. Rita whom she had invoked when she fell into the river.

In the year 1530, Bartolomeo, the son of Giacomo, a native of Colforcella, who fell into a well, was saved through the intercession of St. Rita.

And in the year 1539, St. Rita also saved the life of a little boy who had fallen into a deep well, where he remained three hours before he was discovered.

St. Rita is also powerful against the ravages of earthquakes. In the year 1730, the city of Cascia was in a state of great anxiety and dismay. Hundreds of people from the outlying towns and villages came hurrying into the city to take refuge in the church of St. Rita, frightened by an earthquake, which in a few moments of time, had destroyed many houses. At the very first trembling of the earth in Cascia, the body of St. Rita elevated itself in the coffin, and to the great joy of the frightened people who had sought the aid and protection of the saint, the earthquake ceased without doing any damage.

These and many more miracles, which we could mention, prove that God has endowed the humble Augustinian nun, Sister St. Rita of Cascia, with a wonderful power of obtaining for her clients every and any good thing they desire, and of protecting them from every danger of body and soul.

CHAPTER XXXII.

THE SOLEMN BEATIFICATION OF ST. RITA

WHEN Pope Urban VIII was Bishop of Spoleto, he had numerous occasions to admire some of the prodigies which took place through the intercession of St. Rita. As Cascia belonged to his diocese, he visited the city, at least, once a year, and as he was a very devout client of St. Rita, he never failed to go to her tomb to venerate her holy body. After he had been elevated to the papacy, the holy man did not forget St. Rita. Convinced, personally, of her sanctity, he ordered the cardinals who composed the Sacred Congregation of Rites, to make a thorough examination of the life of St. Rita, with a view to her Beatification. On the 14th of October, in the year of our Lord 1626, the Holy Father sent letters Apostolic to Monsignor Castrucci, bishop of Spoleto, instructing him to prepare the Process, and naming him Commissary Judge; and to Monsignor Colangeli, pronotary Apostolic, who opened the process the 19th day of the same month. The others who were present at the process were: Antonio Raimondo and Francesco Venanci of Cascia, as pronotaries; Father Venancio Pamfili, D. D., advocate and procurator for the nuns; Giovanni Citadini and Leonardi Gregoretti, of Cascia, as procurator deputies for the city of Cascia; and Father Basilio Simonetti and Father

Giovanni Battista di Domenico, procurators for the convent of St. Augustine.

The nuns, of the convent of St. Rita, believing that the time was come when their sister Rita should enjoy a worship approved by the Church, gave strength to their belief, by sending to the Holy Father one of the bees that lived in the convent at Cascia, a descendant, as it were, of the white bees which had appeared at Rita's birth, predicting not only her sanctity, but also that this sanctity would be made known to the entire world by a pope who would be known by the bees. Allusion is here made to the three bees that are to be seen on the Coat of Arms of the Barbarini family, of which Urban VIII was a descendant. The Holy Father was pleased with the courtesy, and blessed the bees, in the person of their little companion, and sent it back to the convent in Cascia.

When the process of the life of St. Rita was concluded and reviewed by the Sacred Congregation of Rites, it was the opinion of the Congregation, that the virtues and miracles of the saint were even greater than what fame and reputation attributed to her. The Congregation therefore approved the finding of the Apostolic Commission. Accordingly, the Holy Father not only approved the worship that the saint had received from the time of her death, but also at the instance of the superioress and the nuns of the convent of St. Rita, granted, on the 2nd of October, in the year 1627, the glorious privilege to the priests of the Augustinian Order, in the diocese of Spoleto, to say Mass and recite office in honor of St. Rita, and to the nuns of the same Order the privilege of reciting office in honor of the saint. On the 4th of February, in the year 1628, at the instance of the Prior General of the Order of St. Augustine, the privilege of saying Mass in honor of St. Rita in any Augustinian church and convent or in any church in the diocese of Spoleto, on the feast of the saint, was extended to the priests of the secular clergy. Ten months after the Apostolic approbation of public worship in honor of St. Rita, the ceremony of her solemn Beatification took place, her name was enrolled in the catalogue of the Blessed, and recorded in the Roman Martyrology.

That the reader may have an idea of the ceremonies attending the Beatification of a servant of God, we will, in as few words as possible, sketch them. Though the ceremonies attending Beatification are not so grand and magnificent as those in connection with Canonization, still they are not wanting in grandeur and solemnity.

On the day appointed for the Beatification, the cardinals who compose the Sacred Congregation of Rites assemble in the Vatican. There are also present large delegations of religious, priests and nuns. The secular clergy is also represented, and you must add to these a multitude of the devout and pious laity. There is no need of decorations in the Vatican to add beauty to the scene. Christian art is everywhere in evidence in the Vatican. The genius of a Michael Angelo and a Raphael has already decorated the Vatican. The ceremonies of the Beatification begin with the reading of the Apostolic Brief declaring the servant of God a Blessed. After the reading of the Brief, a solemn high Mass is sung. The celebrant of the Mass is a bishop Consultor of the Sacred Congregation of Rites. During the Mass, at the intonation of the "Gloria," a large picture of the Blessed, which is on the altar covered with a heavy veil, is uncovered, and exposed to the view of the congregation. The ceremonies end with the chanting of the hymn, "Holy God we praise thy name."

CHAPTER XXXIII.

Festivities Held at Rome and Cascia in Honor of the Solemn Beatification of St. Rita

AS SOON as the Holy See had approved the worship, of which, from the time of her death, St. Rita was the object; and had granted to the priests of the Augustinian Order, the privilege of saying Mass and Office in honor of St. Rita, and to the nuns of the same Order the privilege of the Office; there were held at Rome and at Cascia, solemn and festive celebrations in honor of St. Rita, on the 22nd day of May, in the year of our Lord 1628. On that ever memorable day, the church of St. Augustine at Rome was dressed in its best and most magnificent holiday attire. The facade of the church was decorated with the Papal colors, the Arms of the Augustinian Order, and Papal Arms hung side by side with the Barbarini Arms, of which three bees, as we have already observed, form a part. The interior of the church was also decorated appropriate to the joyful occasion, while the main altar was illuminated with hundreds of lighted wax candles. The church was crowded with devout people, for the name and the fame of St. Rita's sanctity was not unknown in Rome. A solemn high Mass was sung. During the Mass, after the first Gospel, a sermon, detailing the life and virtues of St. Rita, was preached, and when Mass was concluded, the choir, composed of priests, professed clerics and novices of the monastery of St. Augustine, chanted a "Te Deum" in thanksgiving to God for having given to the Church, and for the greater honor and glory of the Order of St. Augustine, so great an ornament as the blessed nun, St. Rita of Cascia.

But grand and solemn as was the celebration in honor of St. Rita, at Rome, the celebration, at Cascia, outstripped in solemnity, grandeur, and magnificence the best efforts of Rome. The people of Cascia, prompted by their love and devotion to St. Rita, had been preparing for a long time to honor her publicly and in a manner never to be forgotten. In fact, they had begun preparations when the process for her Beatification began. The expressed approbation of the Holy See of St. Rita's virtues and sanctity found an echo in the heart of every person in Cascia, and never was the feast day of a saint welcomed with more holy enthusiasm, than the festival day of St. Rita.

The well-to-do people of Cascia decorated the church of the nuns, both inside and outside, with rich bunting and tapestries of silk, and they also had nineteen pictures painted on canvas, each picture representing some event in the life of the saint. Evenings before the feast day, every house in Cascia was ablaze with candles lighting in windows, while pious hands lighted bonfires on the peaks of the highest mountains and hills in and around Cascia, inviting, as it were, with tongues of fire all the neighboring peoples, to come and join in the festival. And at the same time, every bell in Cascia, and in the territory adjacent to Cascia rang out a joyous and hearty invitation to come to do honor to St. Rita.

When the feast of St. Rita came, Cascia was crowded with visitors, who had come from all parts of Italy to be present at the celebration. On all sides could be heard the ***Evviva Santa Rita da Cascia, Hail St. Rita of Cascia,*** of the young as well as of the old. Never before or since has Cascia seen so many clergy, secular and regular within its walls. Naturally, there were a large number of Augustinian priests and nuns present, for they considered St. Rita their sister, by reason of her profession; but both secular and regular vied with one another, in their desires to honor the humble Augustinian nun whom God had honored through His vicegerent on earth.

One thing, however, happened that might have marred all the glory of the celebration, had not the power of St. Rita intervened. On the eve of the feast, when the time came to recite the first vespers of the Office of the saint, the secular clergy claimed the right to conduct the function. The Augustinian priests disputed this right with much vigor. Even the laity entered into the verbal strife, and for a time it looked as if the disputants would come to blows.

The nuns frightened by the commotion caused by the quarrel, implored God, through the intercession of their sainted sister Rita, to pacify the disputants, and to their great surprise, the body of the saint raised itself to the top of the coffin, and opened its eyes which had been closed since the time of the saint's death, a period of 171 years. Astonished at this prodigy, the nuns rang the convent bell, and in answer to the call, thousands passed before the body of St. Rita and were eye witnesses of the prodigy. By reason of this miracle, peace was restored among the disputing clergy. The friars ceded their right to the secular clergy, who chanted the first vespers of the saint, with great devotion, accompanied by the sweet and melodious tones of the organ.

The next day, the feast day of St. Rita, the parish priests of the neighboring towns and villages, marched into Cascia at the head of their congregations, each member of the congregation, carrying in his or her hand, a wax candle ornamented with a piece of silver money, as an offering to the saint. When all the different congregations were assembled, a procession was formed, headed by three hundred persons who carried lighted wax torches, significant of the fire of love and devotion that was burning in their hearts for St. Rita. Many in the procession were dressed as penitents and many were also dressed to represent different saints.

After the procession, Mass was celebrated, after which second Vespers and Complin were chanted. The magnates of the city, the mayor and his council and the aldermen were present and occupied seats in the sanctuary, while the church was filled to overflowing with the faithful of both sexes, who had come to honor and venerate the body of the saint. In the afternoon there was a representation of the "Penitent King David" in a theatre built for the occasion in the largest square in the city.

Before the festival day had come to a close, another miracle, for the greater glory of God and the greater honor of St. Rita, was wrought in the presence of a great multitude. A woman, who belonged to a distinguished and influential family of Spoleto, had been, for many years, under the power and tyranny of an evil spirit. Inspired with confidence, that through the intercession of St. Rita she would obtain from God freedom from her tormentor, she came to Cascia with a number of her relatives and friends. Forcing her way through the multitude that crowded the church, she approached near to the tomb of St. Rita, and after praying for a short time, she was liberated from the evil spirit.

Long after the last visiting congregation had departed for their homes, there could be heard the distant sound of their voices saying: *Evviva, Santa Rita da Cascia.* Though hundreds of years have gone by since the piety of the people of Cascia first uttered these words, they are still repeated today in every land and in every clime wherever there is an Augustinian monastery or convent. *Evviva Santa Rita da Cascia—Hail St. Rita of Cascia.*

CHAPTER XXXIV.

Miracles Wrought by St. Rita After Her Beatification

BESIDES the very many miracles that St. Rita wrought after her death, up to the time of her Beatification, she also wrought many after her Beatification. We will mention a few of the principal ones in this chapter.

Among the many miracles which St. Rita wrought after her Beatification, we must not forget to mention her care in providing, on many occasions, for the necessities of the nuns of her convent in Cascia. One day, Sister Costanza, the superioress of the convent, was sorely perplexed and troubled, because there was not a drop of wine in the convent, nor had she the money to buy it. With all confidence she went to the tomb of St. Rita, and made known her want to the saint. A short time afterwards, the superioress heard a loud knock at the door of the convent. When the door was opened, a man stood without and said he had a barrel of wine for the convent. When the wine was put in the cellar, the man disappeared suddenly, as well as the donkey and the cart which had brought the supply of wine.

On another occasion, the same superioress experienced the same want. St. Rita again came to her aid.

Signora Petrangeli, the esteemed wife of the treasurer of Cascia, sent some wine to the convent. In a note she informed the superioress, that for three successive nights, while sleeping, she heard St. Rita saying to her: "Send some wine to the convent, the nuns have none."

Another superioress was in urgent need of money to pay a bill. She invoked the aid of St. Rita. That very day, the superioress found in the almsbox the necessary aid and assistance.

Not only has St. Rita aided the nuns of her convent in their temporal affairs, but she has also been most solicitous about their spiritual necessities. Father Gregorio Anselmi of Offida, who had been the confessor of the nuns of Cascia for ten years, and afterwards subprior of St. Augustine's monastery in Rome, relates, that, on many occasions, when a nun fell dangerously ill, he heard in his sleep a voice saying repeatedly: "Father Confessor!" Awakened by the voice, which he believed to be St. Rita's, he would scarcely be dressed, when a messenger from the convent would come, in all haste, and tell him, that one of the nuns was dangerously ill, and was calling for him.

The same priest relates that Sister Elizabetta, one of the nuns, who had been ill with catarrh for some time, became weak, one night, and called for her confessor. Both the physician and the superioress, judging there was not the least danger of death, were loath to send for him since the hour was very late. However, the superioress did send word, but informed him that the call was not urgent, so he did not go. The next morning, while saying Mass, he felt as if there was a voice telling him to hasten to see the sick nun. After Mass he went immediately to the bed-side of the patient, and found her actually dying. Scarcely had he administered the last Sacraments, than her soul departed for heaven to receive its eternal reward. Before dying, Sister Elizabetta said it was St. Rita who had sent the Father Confessor to her bedside, so that she would not die without the last Sacraments.

In the year 1658, a few days before the feast of St. Rita, a woman, who happened to be in the church, noticed that the lamp before the saint's tomb was not lighting. She hastened, at once, and informed the sister sacristan, who could scarcely believe what the woman said, since she herself had lighted the lamp at early morn. Going to the tomb, she found to her great surprise, that the taper in the lamp was extinguished. She then went to the sacristy to get a lighter, but on returning, to her greater surprise, she found the lamp had been lighted without the intervention of human hands. This fact was authenticated before Giuseppe Benatti, notary public, the 16th of July, in the year 1660.

Filippo Antonio Gregoretti, a native of Macerata, was at the point of death, by reason of a malady that had afflicted him for many years. Full of confidence in the intercession of St. Rita, he asked her to ask God to cure him. His recourse to St. Rita was not in vain, he was restored to health. Filippo himself wrote to the superioress of the convent of Cascia, on the 10th of May, in the year of our Lord 1661, and informed her of the miraculous cure he had obtained through the intercession of St. Rita.

And finally, among the many more wonders that God wrought, through the intercession of St. Rita we will make mention of the following. There lived in the city of Gublio, in the province of Umbria, a gentleman, named Persio Piasi and his wife Cecilia. Both were of distinguished and illustrious families, the possessors of much wealth, and better than all, they were pious and devout Christians. They had lived together happily for eighteen years, but God had not blessed their union with any children. As they both desired an heir to their name and wealth, they had recourse to the intercession of St. Rita and were consoled. A beautiful son was born to them, and one of the names they gave him was Rita, for they considered their little son as the fruit of the intercession of St. Rita.

CHAPTER XXXV.

The Rapid Spread of Devotion to St. Rita

LONG before the time of her solemn Beatification, devotion to St. Rita of Cascia had begun. At first, in the province of Umbria; thence it spread to every province in Italy, and then flew, as it were, on the wings of love across the Mediterranean Sea and planted itself in the kingdom of Spain. After her Beatification, however, so rapid was the propagation of the devotion, that in every part of Europe wherever there was an Augustinian Church, Monastery or convent, there also could be found an altar or shrine dedicated to Sister St. Rita of Cascia.

Devotion to St. Rita did not long confine itself exclusively to Europe. In the course of time, zealous and devout Augustinian missionaries brought the devotion across the broad Atlantic ocean, and it was not long before the peoples of Spanish America vied in their devotion to St. Rita, not only with their kindred in the mother country, but also with their brethren in Italy.

From the annals of the Order of St. Augustine we learn, that when Father Diego de los Rios was elected provincial of the Province of the Holy Name of Jesus in Mexico, on the 6th day of May, in the year 1645, one of the first things he did was to introduce, with great fervor and zeal, devotion to St. Rita in the City of

Mexico. Time has added new zeal to this devotion, for even to this day the faithful of Mexico City, in spite of all the machinations of secret societies to root up and destroy their faith, so love and venerate the memory of the holy Augustinian nun, that they consider her their patron and advocate. Another proof of the love of the Mexicans for our saint, is that the majority of their little daughters receive, at baptism, the name of Rita.

Devotion to St. Rita took root and flourished also in Flascala. Flascala was before its conversion to Christianity, a most powerful republic. Today it is a "privileged city" of Indians, in reward for the valor of their ancestors who were faithful allies of the Spaniards in the conquest of Mexico. In the parish church of Flascala, there is a magnificent altar, surrounded by a forest of elegant columns, with plinths and capitals of burnished gold dedicated to St. Rita. Every year her feast day is celebrated with much pomp and solemnity.

A special mention must be made of the piety and liberality of the clients of St. Rita who builded a beautiful cathedral in her honor in the city, formerly called San Sebastian, now Rio Janeiro. This cathedral enjoys many privileges granted by a decree of Pope Benedict XIII, dated the 17th day of September, in the year of our Lord 1724.

Thus we see that the devotion to St. Rita, which had its beginning in Cascia, the very day of the saint's death, soon spread over Europe, and carried, so to speak, by the winds that roam the broad Atlantic, found a home in the pious hearts of the faithful of South America.

Like the people of Italy, the people of Spain venerated St. Rita as a saint, long before she was Beautified; and so many and so great were the favors they received from God through the intercession of the saint, that the faithful of Spain were the first to call St. Rita: *Advocate of the Impossible.* In fact, it was the pious people of Valencia, where that grand ornament of the Catholic Church, our own St. Thomas of Villanova, ruled as bishop for many years, who gave this title to our saint. To the people of Cadiz, however, belongs the honor of calling St. Rita: *Saint of impossible things;* and it is by this title that St. Rita, the humble Augustinian nun of Cascia is universally known.

That Sister St. Rita merits the title of *Saint of the Impossible* there can be no doubt. A retrospect of her life and and the prodigies she wrought after her death will emphasize her undoubted right to the title.

She was born when her parents had reached that age which excludes all hope of offspring, unless by a singular favor from God.

A swarm of white bees humming and buzzing around her cradle, entering and issuing forth from her tiny mouth, predicted that sweetness of disposition, speech, and manners, which was to be one of the striking characteristics of her life.

As a maiden she was a mirror of innocence and purity—a lily among thorns. Her married life was signalized, not only by converting a wayward and iracible husband into a docile and loving companion, but also by a conjugal chastity that was wonderful.

Her marvellous entrance into the convent, though the doors were securely locked and the windows barred. Her wonderful patience in suffering for fifteen years the pains of the wound, on her forehead, caused by the sacred thorn.

Though she lived to a ripe age, she ate little, and punished her body with a rigorous and continual penance. She caused flowers and fruits to bloom and grow in the midst of the snow and ice of an inclement winter. After death, she raised her body to the top of the coffin, and opened her eyes as if she were living and not dead.

Finally, the numberless miracles wrought through her intercession, in favor of those who had recourse to her in their difficulties and afflictions when all human aid failed them, tell us plainly that Sister St. Rita of Cascia merits the title: *Saint of Impossible things.*

How graphically is not the life of St. Rita crystalized in that beautiful hymn, which the Augustinian friars and nuns recite, at office, each year in honor of St. Rita on her feast day, May 22nd:

Come, virgins chaste, pure brides, draw near:
Let each exult and Heaven hear
The hymn which grateful accents raise,
Our song of joy in Rita's praise.

By fast her sinless frame is weak;
Her livid flesh the scourges streak.
In pity for her Savior's woes,
Her days and even nights are closed.

The thorn-wound on her brow is shown,
The crimson rose in winter blown,
And full-ripe figs in frozen tree
At Rita's wish the wonderers see.

The widowed spouse and wedded wife
The way to Heaven see in her life;
The way secure our Rita trod,
In life's dim day, through pain to God.

Praise to the Father and the Son,
Praise to the Spirit, Three in One;
O grant us grace in Heaven to reign
Through Rita's prayer and life-long pain.

CHAPTER XXXVI.

The Solemn Canonization of St. Rita

THE UNIVERSAL and uninterrupted devotion of the faithful to St. Rita, and the very many wonderful prodigies that God wrought through her intercession, enkindled, in the loving hearts of thousands and thousands of the clients of the humble Augustinian nun, the ardent desire of seeing her elevated to that highest honor, with which Holy Mother Church recompenses the heroic virtues of her pious and devout children. This ardent desire began to manifest itself shortly after her Beatification. However, generation after generation of the devout clients of St. Rita went to their reward, without seeing the realization of their wishes. But at length the happy time came after a lapse of two centuries of years and more. The year 1900 will long be remembered by the friars and nuns of the Order of St. Augustine, as well as by the loving and devout clients of St. Rita. In this year, on the 24th of May, Pope Leo XII, of happy memory, decreed that Blessed Rita, O. S. A., of Cascia should be honored as a saint, in public and in private; that her name be inscribed in the catalogue of the saints, and that her memory should be held in perpetual veneration on the 22nd day of May each year by the Universal Church.

We will mention some of the details that anteceded the Canonization of St. Rita. In the year 1737, a few years more than a century after her Beatification, the Apostolic Process of the virtues and particularly of the miracles of St. Rita was begun. This Process was conducted by the diocesan tribunals of Spoleto and Nursia. For different reasons, some particular, some general, the Process was delayed for more than a century. On the 9th of September, in the year 1851, letters were sent from Rome to the bishop of Nursia to reopen and complete the Process. The procedure lasted four years. In 1855 the Process was sent to Rome, approved the following year by the Sacred Congregation of Rites, and confirmed by a decree of Pope Pius IX, the 29th of May, in the year 1856. On June 8th, in the year of our Lord 1896, the Sacred Congregation approved the Process made in the year 1626 of the sanctity, virtues, and worship to the saint, thereby giving it the value of an Apostolic Process. On April 6th, in the year 1897, the same Congregation approved the Process of the virtues of St. Rita, and declared that steps could be taken, at once, to examine the miracles attributed to the saint. After a long and careful examination as the Church is accustomed to do in such cases, Pope Leo XIII, by a decree dated Palm Sunday, April 8th, in the year 1900, approved, among the many, the miracles attributed to St. Rita, and declared that they could, with all security, proceed to the solemn Canonization of the saint. The following were the three miracles that were approved, as we may learn from the Decree of St. Rita's Canonization.

"The first miracle consists of that pleasing scent emanating from the remains of the Saint's body, the existence of which is confirmed by many reliable witnesses and trustworthy tradition, so that to doubt concerning this fact would be absurd; moreover no natural cause can be given for the existence of this odor, as we see from the physical research which has been made by men most skilled in such things. Furthermore this odor diffuses itself in a manner above the usual laws of nature. Hence we should be persuaded that this fragrance has its origin through divine intervention."

"The other miracle happened to Elizabeth Bergamini, a young girl in danger of losing her sight from smallpox. Her parents assured by the physicians that the child's condition was so serious, that medical aid could be of no avail, decided to send her to the Augustinian Convent at Cascia, beseeching St. Rita fervently to deliver their daughter from approaching blindness. Arriving at the convent, the child was clothed with a votive dress in honor of St. Rita. After four months Elizabeth cried out one day that she could see. Together with the nuns she immediately began to give thanks to God who had wrought such a miracle through St. Rita."

"The third miracle happened to Cosimo Pelligrini, suffering from chronic catarrhal gastro-enteritis and hemorhoidal affection so serious that there was no hope of recovery. Returning one day from church he became so weak from a new attack of his excruciating malady, that he was near death. Doctors, being summoned, ordered him to receive the last Sacraments, receiving which he lay in the bed with every appearance of approaching death, when suddenly he seemed to see St. Rita in the attitude of greeting him. Thereupon his former strength and appetite returned to him, and within a very short time he was able to do the work of a young man, although he was advanced in years, being a septuagenerian."

In consideration of the approval of the virtues and miracles of the humble Augustinian nun, Pope Leo XIII issued the Decree of Canonization, and appointed Ascension Day, May 24th, 1900, for the happy event. On this memorable day, two blessed servants of God were canonized. Blessed John Baptist de La Salle, Founder of the Brothers of the Christian Schools, and our own Blessed Rita of Cascia, known throughout the entire Catholic world as the *Saint of the Impossible.*

On that occasion there was present a large multitude of people. Pilgrims had come from Ireland, England, France, Germany, Spain, America and from every province in Italy to witness the rarest and most solemn ceremonies of Holy Church. In preparation for the canonization, more than 1500 persons were employed under the direction of Constantine Sneider who had charge of the decorations of the Vatican. It was on this occasion, that electric light was used for the first time in St. Peter's Church. Nearly 11,000,000 feet of wire supplied the current for 12,000 lamps and 400 chandeliers.

At an early hour of the morning of May 24th, 1900, there was assembled in the plaza of St. Peter an immense multitude of people of every nationality and language, indicating that the entire world was represented. The front of St. Peter's Church stood forth in all its majestic beauty, enhanced by the splendor of its gorgeous and magnificent decorations.

In the meantime, there were assembled in the Vatican Palace awaiting the beginning of the ceremonies: the Sacred College of Cardinals; Patriarchs; Archbishops and Bishops; Regular Clergy: the Chapter

Fathers of Basilicas and Colleges; the Parish priests of Rome; and by special privilege, the students of the Roman and French seminaries.

At precisely eight o'clock, His Sanctity, accompanied by his Court of Nobles, proceeded to the Sistine Chapel where the College of Cardinals, the Archbishops and Bishops and all those who were to take part in the pontifical function were awaiting his arrival. After the hymn *Ave Maris Stella* was chanted, the Holy Father knelt for a few moments in prayer, and then ascended the Chair of State—Sedia Gestatoria—to accompany the procession to the Basilica of St. Peter. The procession was composed of three divisions. The first division had in its ranks the Regular Clergy. Among others Calced and Discalced Augustinians; Brothers of the Christian Schools; Cophuchins; Carmelites; Dominicans, Benedictines, and Canons of St. John Lateran. The second division was made up of Secular Clergy. The Parish-priests of Rome; Canons of the Basilicas and Collegiate Churches of Rome; Officials, Priests and Prelates and Consultors of the Sacred Congregation of Rites. The third division was composed of the Pontifical Court; the Chaplains and Chamberlains; Procurator Generals of Religious Orders; Auditors and Relators of the Roman Rota; Archbishops, Bishops and Cardinals. The Holy Fathers, Borne on the Chair of State, followed, surrounded by the Commanders and Chiefs of the Noble Guards; the Swiss Guards; the Palatines and the Prior Generals of Religious Orders. It was half past ten o'clock when the Holy Father arrived in St. Peter's Church and the ceremonies of Canonization began. The Decree of Canonization setting forth the apostolic sentence, was read. High Mass was sung by Cardinal Oreglia, Dean of the Sacred College.

The music was under the direction of Maestro Mustafa, Director of the Sistine Choir. When the Mass was concluded, the Holy Father gave the Papal Benediction, and then retired to his room in the Vatican Palace amid loud huzzahs of love and affection, as the people repeated again and again: "Long live Leo XIII." Rome was then, as it is today, under the rule and in the hands of a descendant of a robber king, but the ceremonies which had just terminated proved that Rome was still, as it is today, the City of the Popes, and the Metripolitan of triumphant Catholicity.

CHAPTER XXXVII.

CONCLUSION

WE HAVE observed, that ardent and fervent devotion to St. Rita of Cascia has flourished in Europe and Spanish America for hundreds of years. In less than a dozen years this devotion has taken so deep a root in the hearts of the faithful of North America, that devout clients of St. Rita are to be found in every large city of theUnited States. In the East, there are shrines erected in honor of St. Rita in New York, Brooklyn, Albany, Buffalo, Philadelphia, Boston, Worcester and Lawrence. In the West, St. Rita has shrines in Dallas, Denver and in our own city of Chicago.

Devotion to St. Rita was introduced to the faithful of Chicago by Very Rev. J. F. Green, O. S. A., Rector of St. Rita's church, located at the corner of 63rd street and Oakley avenue. In the church is an humble shrine of the saint, and the large concourse of people who visit the shrine every Thursday, accentuates the fact, that St. Rita of Cascia, the humble Augustinian nun, is loved and venerated by thousands and thousands of the faithful who come from all parts of Chicago to invoke the intercession of the *Saint of the Impossible* and to kiss her relic.

During the Novena to St. Rita which begins each year on the 13th day of May and concludes May 22nd the feast day of the saint, so great is the multitude of people that attend the devotions, which begin at early morn and continue till late in the evening, that one would imagine he was at Lourdes, France, or at the shrine of the Mother of Good Counsel at Benazzano, Italy, or at Compostela, in Spain. Father Green is in receipt of a score of letters every week, testifying to the many favors and graces obtained through the intercession of St. Rita.

We will now conclude the story of the life of Sister St. Rita by quoting the tenor of the concluding words of the Decree of Canonization.

The solemn honors that Holy Mother Church confers on her saints, should fill, with supreme joy, the hearts of the faithful, and move them efficaciously to the imitation of those virtues which made the Saints beautiful and pleasing to Jesus Christ, the King of saints. St. Rita of Cascia, as maid, wife, mother, and nun, was so pleasing and so beloved by Jesus Christ, that He deigned to signalize her, not only with the seal of His love, but especially with the seal of His Passion. St. Rita merited this great privilege on account of her singular humility, her entire detachment from the things of earth, and by an admirable penance during the different stages of her wonderful life. However, the virtues which made St. Rita particularly pleasing to God were her love for her neighbor and her affection and devotion to Jesus Christ crucified. The two virtues contain all the wisdom of Christianity. St. Rita recommends us to practice these two virtues. Let us, therefore, invoke her as our intercessor, so that by the constant exercise of these two virtues, which go hand in hand, we may be able to preserve with honor, both the sanctity and the dignity of the glorious name of Christians.

CPSIA information can be obtained
at www.ICGtesting.com
Printed in the USA
LVHW042254051222
734629LV00012B/863

9 781376 232585